ANNA B. MOW

FIND YOUR OWN FAITH

ZONDERVAN
PUBLISHING HOUSE

Mow, Anna B
   Find your own faith.

   1. Bible—Study.   I. Title.
BS600.2.M65   230   77-23821
ISBN 0-310-29652-8

FIND YOUR OWN FAITH!
© 1977 by The Zondervan Corporation
Grand Rapids, Michigan

Second printing   November 1977

Unless indicated otherwise, Scripture references are from the Revised Standard Version, copyright © 1946, 1952 by the Division of Christian Education of the National Council of Churches of Christ in the United States of America

Printed in the United States of America

CONTENTS

I pray that your inward eyes may be illumined, *so that you may know what is the hope to which he calls you, what the wealth and glory of the share he offers you among his people in their heritage, and how vast the resources of his power open to us who trust in him.*
(Ephesians 1:18,19 NEB)

We speak of these gifts of God in words found for us not by our human wisdom but by the Spirit. A man who is unspiritual refuses what belongs to the Spirit of God; it is folly to him; he cannot grasp it, because it needs to be judged in the light of the Spirit.
(1 Corinthians 2:13,14 NEB)

PREFACE

When faith gets shaky, doubt usually begins with questions about the Bible.

Recently, while at a retreat in a church college, a student asked to talk with me. I had taught her father in seminary, so I was especially interested in her. Dolefully she said, "I can no longer accept the faith my father taught me." Apparently she expected an argument from me, as she was surprised when I said, "That's all right. You are old enough now to have your own faith, one that is more than an imitation faith, which was all right when you were a child." She relaxed, and we were free to talk about what real faith is.

Kenneth's parents had helped him to grow into a mature faith of his own. He was not upset by all the new ideas he heard in college. The content of his faith began to change somewhat, but he was not emotionally disturbed because no walls had been built into his life against new ideas. Therefore, every new interpretation was an adventure to him. Then Kenneth spent a summer in a church camp where he attended a Bible class. This Bible teacher thought himself a scholar, but he had the absurd notion that he must ridicule any idea a student already had in order to make room for new ideas. Kenneth's faith was shaken for the first time in his life. He came home saying, "My mind is tired and my soul is sick."

There is enough frustration in this world without deliberately creating more. I cannot understand why, in an age of specially trained counselors, any intelligent person would *deliberately* upset youth. A good counselor or teacher begins where the person is and leads him from there to deeper truth.

We must stay open to learn more about truth, God's truth. We begin, as the Bible does, with *faith in the fact of a living God*. We keep open minds, not empty minds. If God created the world, all truth is God's truth. The more we learn about the discoveries of science, the greater our conception of God will become. Some people have been so dried up in their attitude toward the Bible that they miss the life it reveals. They use the Bible to prove their own ideas rather than coming to the Bible to find truth God has for them. We don't have to prove the truth; we find it and proclaim it. The greatest adventure in life is to find out about God and to obey Him. That is what we want to do as we consider the Bible, for it is the story of the living God who takes the initiative toward man to have relationship with him. And we begin our adventure with excitement, not with fear. *All aboard!*

Some of the chapters in this book were first published in my book *Your Experience and the Bible*. Since I now have full rights to that material, I put it back where it came from in this manuscript. (My thanks to Clayton Carlson for this privilege.)

I would like to express my deep appreciation to Genie Price for reading and correcting my words, to Judy Markham for her efficient editing, and to Cecile Dowdy for her final typing.

And my deepest gratitude to our living Lord and Savior, Jesus Christ.

OLD TESTAMENT — *God is*.
NEW TESTAMENT — *God is Love*.

1
PREPARATION FOR THE ADVENTURE

There is power in this Book called the Word of God, and I am intrigued by what happens to people who come to it with open minds and hearts, or even with mere curiosity, when it is honest.

Moy Gwong came from Canton, China, to Chicago to work in a laundry. A friend brought him to a Chinese Sunday school where he could learn English. He was also given a New Testament in his own language. That very night he started to read, and he could not lay it down. By daybreak he was at the end of the Book of Revelation, and he had a revelation. When he returned to the church the next Sunday, he asked for baptism. The pastor was sure this man could not be ready to be a Christian, but after examining him through an interpreter, he was satisfied and baptized him. After Moy Gwong had learned English, he went

11

through high school, college, and seminary and then returned to his village in China as a missionary.

A young Polish rabbi on his first reading of the forbidden book, the New Testament, accepted Jesus as his Messiah. He was disinherited and fled across Europe to America where he finally became a minister and a New Testament professor in a theological seminary in the United States.

John Subhan at thirteen was a recognized Moslem mystic. A copy of the Gospel According to Matthew came into his hands. He read it several times and then went to his parents and said, "I am a Christian." They were shocked and threatened him. He stood firm and was cast out of his home. For three weeks he walked the streets of Calcutta looking up into the face of every foreigner until he found a man who looked like he knew the Good News. The man did know — he was a missionary. John was baptized and grew in the Lord. He is now a retired Methodist bishop.

Sadly, there are even more people who have grown up knowing about the Bible but who have been blinded to its real message by those who are so adamant in their own interpretations that they turn even sincere seekers of truth against the Bible, or at least make them indifferent to it. Our struggle is to be strong in conviction but at the same time open to new truth. The truth is so great we can never know it all.

Sue had been upset for some time by theological conflicts to which she had been exposed. I was in her home when she was recuperating from the flu, so we had plenty of time to visit. After all the talking we had done, I was surprised on Saturday morning when she said, ''I want to talk to you, and I want daddy present.'' So as we sat in the breakfast nook, she burst out, ''I don't believe in the virgin birth. I don't believe in the Resurrection. I don't believe — '' I interrupted her because I wanted her to get into a positive attitude so she would be *able* to change her views. I said, ''Sue, I don't care what you don't believe. Tell me what you *do* believe, and we'll start from there.'' She was surprised because she expected me to be shocked.

Soon Sue relaxed and began to talk about what she did believe. Then I could say, ''Now stand on what you do believe, look around at the things you question, and use the good mind God gave you to discern the truth.'' When I left Sue at the airport later, her last words were, ''So I stand on the things I do believe and look around at the things I am not sure of!''

That was in February. On the following Easter Sue wrote, ''Yesterday daddy was the last one to leave the church. (He is the pastor.) A bush in front of the church was on fire. This was dangerous for our wooden church. Daddy ran for a fire extinguisher. . . . I wonder what would have happened if he had taken off his shoes instead of running for the fire extinguisher! Suppose Moses had known about fire extinguishers!'' Sue is coming along. Her God-given good humor is helping her on the way to new truth.

A teacher asked a Bible class, ''Is the God of the Old Testament the same as the God of the New Testament?'' A student answered, ''Of course, 'God is the same yesterday and today and for ever.' '' An older man, always on the lookout for anything "unorthodox," exclaimed, "That is not right. It is '*Jesus Christ* the same yesterday and today and for ever.' " The teacher responded, "Thank you for the correction, because it is only through Jesus that we know that the God of the Old Testament is the same as the God of the New Testament."

God is the same through all the centuries. What is more surprising is that people are much the same through all the generations and around the world. In Indian villages, where a white woman had never been seen before, I was surprised to find real fellowship. The people there may have been illiterate, but they were not unintelligent. And they were real people, wise in the matters of life. When many of them learned to know God, we could have even deeper fellowship. This gave me a new understanding of the people in the Bible. They, too, were *people* worshiping the *same God* and having a similar relationship with Him.

I must conclude then that the God who called Abraham and Moses and spoke to and through the prophets is the same God who wants to lead me and make His will known to me. Thus, I cannot understand the story of God's relationship with those people of ancient days unless I come to their story with the same openness of mind and heart that they had.

To understand inspired Scripture I must be inspired by the same Spirit. I cannot understand the faith of Abraham unless I come to his story with the same faith he had. I cannot identify with the apostle Paul unless I have a similar relationship with the Lord Jesus

14

Christ. I may not reach Paul's depth, but I can have the same commitment. Identification with the people of the Bible in experience of God is the secret to understanding the Bible, for faith is the beginning of understanding. They did not question the existence of God; they began with faith in Him — so faith is the secret of understanding.

The people of the Bible were people of other lands, other eras, other cultures. God reached through to them in their own time, in the midst of their own cultures. He had patience with them when they were slow to learn. It is exciting, however, to find the ways in which they did rise above their cultures as they responded to God. Recognizing where they were limited in their human understanding because of their cultures solves for us the difficulties we have in relation to some of the ways of Old Testament people. They wanted and needed children in those days, so if the wife was barren a man was supposed to try to conceive with another woman, as Abraham did with Hagar. Solomon's culture did not limit him in the number of wives he had. Every time he made a peace treaty with another king, he was given a princess as a wife. And he was a man of peace, at least with other nations! We imitate those men of the faith only in areas where they had learned to live *above* their culture.

Many practices that were acceptable in their culture would not be acceptable in our day, but our culture has developed out of centuries of learning. We cannot criticize them unless we live above our culture as much as they lived above theirs.

15

When Jesus and the early Christians quoted Scripture it was, of course, the Old Testament, for Jesus created the New Testament and His followers wrote it under the guidance of the Spirit. We need not be troubled by anything in the Old Testament if we interpret it as they did.

One morning I was reading a book by a French theologian. He said that everything in the Old Testament was inspired to be written. I believed that, but that afternoon I read the Book of Judges. God's chosen people were so wicked; they forgot God over and over again. When they repented, God sent them a deliverer. I got so impatient with them that I felt under a cloud because these horrible stories were written "under inspiration." After I went to bed that night I cried to the Lord, "Why were all these things written in the Word?" Then it dawned on me that the theme of the Bible is not basically the story of man's wickedness. Human wickedness is recognized, but it was written in the light of a God who loved enough to bring redemption.

The Bible is not part of a dead past, because although it shows how God sought us long ago, the same God seeks us in the same ways today. This amazing God-love is just as much a part of the living present. The Bible holds answers to the very questions people are asking today. As we read the Bible honestly, seeking the truth, an amazing thing happens: we become conscious of more than the mere words of a book. We become conscious of a living Presence and sense divine relationship. This is why the Bible is called the Word of

God. Such an experience is the beginning of the most creative thing that can happen to your life. Treasure it and be obedient to every cadence of the Spirit. Obedient faith trains the listening ear so that we can be sure of the "voice of God" for us.

Many "uneducated" people around the world have read the Bible with listening ear and have learned to know God. But this is no argument against education. Remember, God does not ask for an empty mind, only an open one. The more you can learn *about* the Bible and *about* God, the more exciting it becomes. All you need to remember is that getting information for your mind is one thing, but having relationship with a personal God is a matter of *response to Him* with your whole being.

In college, you may take a course on the Bible. There you will see it either as literature or as a history of a people. This should be interesting, even exciting. And you will never "lose your faith" by this study, as so many have done, if you will remember that God's truth is never known by the intellect alone. The Bible was not written as a college textbook, although it makes a good one; it was written to tell how much God wants you and what He wants to do for you.

The Bible was not written as a history book, and it never claimed to be a science text. Whatever history is recorded in it is given only as a framework for the events in the history of God's chosen people. Such events were counted important because through them the people learned to better understand God.

Some scholars in the past have failed to realize that

Bible history is not written like secular history. When any place or person mentioned in the Bible was not found in secular history, they took it for granted that the writers of the Bible made a mistake. I remember the first story I heard concerning this when I was young. A King Sargon is mentioned in Isaiah 20:1, and since no one could find anything about such a king in any other records, they decided there never was a King Sargon in that period of history. Then in 1845 French archaeologists uncovered priceless treasures in the area of old Nineveh. They found tens of thousands of inscriptions of old Assyria, including the story of Sargon II and details of his reign. They even found his record of the battle described in Isaiah 20. So the Bible did not make a mistake after all!

Some church people seem to think that the Bible came in one piece from God and in King James English at that! Our Book did not come in one piece. Our Scriptures were written over a period of a thousand years by men who had listened to God. Actually, the Bible is a library of books, sixty-six in all. For centuries records were not written, but the stories of God's work among men were passed from generation to generation by almost faultless oral tradition.

The first account we have of even a recognition of anything called the Word of God or Scripture was in 621 B.C. Manasseh was a wicked king of Judah. He tried to wipe out all the good things his God-fearing father, Hezekiah, had accomplished. Manasseh reigned fifty-five years and his wicked son two years, and during this time they managed to lead the majority of the people away from the true God of Israel.

Then Josiah, grandson of Manasseh, ascended the throne. Although he was only eight years old, he had good advisors and he listened to them, especially to Hilkiah, the high priest. When he was eighteen, he took his full responsibility as king. His grandfather and father had defiled the temple, so Josiah had it cleansed and restored. During the cleanup Hilkiah found a scroll, a book of the Law. He sent a message to Shaphan, the king's secretary, "I have found the book of the law in the house of the LORD" (2 Kings 22:8). When Shaphan read the book to the king, Josiah tore his clothes in despair. Then he asked the priests to find out from the Lord about the words in the scroll. They took the scroll to Huldah, a prophetess, who verified it as the Word of God. From what followed we can infer that the Scripture was from the Book of Deuteronomy.

Then Josiah began a real cleanup campaign. Every foreign cult object was removed from the temple and destroyed. The temple was no longer a place for the worship of Baal, but was for Yahweh, as they called the Lord God. The prostitutes, who were living in the temple as part of the Baal worship, were banished and their living quarters wrecked. Josiah destroyed every place of Baal worship throughout the land. Child sacrifice was forbidden. (Manasseh had sacrificed one of his own sons to Baal.) Mediums and wizards were outlawed. The people did not change their idolatrous ways overnight, but the king had done all he could.

After the cleanup Josiah prepared for the Passover observance, which he found described in the scroll. It is written that "no such passover had been kept since the days of the judges who judged Israel, or during all the days of the kings of Israel or of the kings of Judah" (2 Kings 23:22).

This was the beginning of an appreciation for the *written* Word of God, but until the time of the Exile, little more was done to gather together the oral traditions and the literature already compiled in the time of King Solomon. Then, when the temple had been destroyed and the people were in captivity, in their despair they began to appreciate what they had lost. As they adjusted to their unhappy circumstances, they began to realize that the heritage of their faith was not dependent upon a special place to worship or political independence. Ezra and other scribes began in earnest to collect and organize their unique literature. They found the stories of God's love and will for His chosen people, and they came to see that they were still God's children even in suffering.

The first record we have of the use of the Pentateuch — the first five books of the Old Testament — is in Nehemiah. After his exile in Persia, Nehemiah came to Jerusalem and helped to rebuild the walls of the city. Then a great celebration was held to praise God for the return of many exiles. At this celebration the Book of the Law was read to the people. Several hours a day for eight days the people listened to God's Word (about 444 B.C.).

This reading of the Law gave new stimulus to respect for the written Word and its value in their religious life. Gradually historical writings, sermons, and the words of the prophets were added to the list. By 200 B.C. the Scriptures were quite well accepted as we know them in the Old Testament. Later, when Jesus spoke of the Scriptures, He was talking about this collection of books in the form of scrolls. Later we will see how Jesus used these Scriptures so we can use them as He did.

The Old Testament was written in Hebrew and the New Testament in Greek. Both were written in the everyday language of the people. Every Bible in any other language is a translation from the original.

I never realized the subtleties of translation until I had to speak through an interpreter in India. We had to learn two languages for our work. I could teach in the first language but not in the second. However, I could understand what my interpreter said, and I could ask and answer questions. My helper had never translated for anyone before. He would take one sentence and translate it literally. By the end of a paragraph my meaning was often missed. He had translated words and did not get the meaning.

After the third day of this, I found a book written in his language that covered some of the things I was teaching. He read the whole book that night. The next day he said to me, "Now I understand what you are trying to teach. Please give me a whole paragraph at a time, and I will interpret it for you." This made it easy for me. I didn't even have to watch my use of English idioms. To explain hoarseness in my throat I might say, "I have a frog in my throat." A *literal* translation of that idiom would make them want to look in my throat to find the frog! To translate the meaning in his language he would say, "My throat sat down." We need the literal *meaning* translated.

We have no *original* texts of any part of the Bible. Until the first Dead Sea Scrolls were found in 1947 (and more later), the oldest text of any part of the Bible was from the 9th century A.D. Every text had been copied from another text, which had been copied from another, etc. It is a miracle that the truth of God's story came through so clearly. But God has given His Word, and He is capable of protecting it.

The most exciting scroll found among the Dead Sea Scrolls was a copy of the whole Book of Isaiah from about 100 B.C. Perhaps Jesus saw that copy! This scroll is a thousand years older than any copy we had before and is kept in a long, glass case around a big pillar in an underground bomb-proof library in Jerusalem. I thanked God for His holy Word as I walked slowly around that pillar and looked at what men had copied by hand even before Jesus lived on this earth.

Although God appears in the Old Testament as a God of history, the basic story is about His relationship with individuals. We want to find out how God reached through to those people of ancient days. We want to know the story of God's chosen people, of their responses and failures, their despairs and hopes. After the last book in the Old Testament, there is an interval of several hundred years until the "fullness of time" when Jesus came with the Good News (the gospel), which is contained in the New Testament.

On the black cover of *Time* for 8 April 1966,

written in large red letters was the question: IS GOD DEAD? Three years later on 26 December 1969, the *Time* cover came in white with sunshine streaks all over it and the new question was: IS GOD COMING BACK TO LIFE?

God has been here all the time, but spiritual blindness kept people from seeing Him. I heard the late modern prophet of Israel, Martin Buber, say some years ago, "God comes in wherever He is let in." We want to know how God comes into man's consciousness and how He can come to us.

2
GOD STARTED IT

*The heavens are telling the glory of God; and the
firmament proclaims his handiwork.*
(Psalm 19:1)

*When I look at thy heavens, the work of thy
fingers, the moon and the stars which thou hast
established;*
*What is man that thou art mindful of him, and the
son of man that thou dost care for him?*
(Psalm 8:3,4)

To understand the biblical story of the Creation
one must begin with praise to God, the Creator, because the Genesis story is written to magnify God.
There were other stories of creation current in the day
the Genesis story was written, but the Bible account is
not an imitation of those other stories. Our story is
unique in that God is its hero. To the people of the Bible

the important fact of creation is that *God started it all*.

Of course, they spoke in terms of the understanding of their day. Why should God give a special revelation about a day to come when a man from the United States would read this creation story from outer space? God created man to discover some things for himself. Special revelation is for the things man cannot find out on his own. Man cannot find God on his own, so the special revelation is for the revelation of God.

The story in Genesis does not tell *how* God created the world or even how long a "day" was, but it does tell us without question that *God did it*. The people who tried to figure out by themselves how everything began developed most fantastic stories. They are interesting, but they are not about God. In fact, the whole Bible is the story of how God revealed Himself to man.

People around the world and through all the ages have been religious in their seeking of ultimate truth, but only in the Bible do we have the story of God taking the initiative toward man. This is what revelation means. It is for relationship. Man's part is basically *responding* to this revelation rather than carrying the full responsibility in a search for God. This is the first basic difference between the religion of the Bible and all other faiths.

So the first sentence in our Bible states, "In the beginning God. . . ." The God who started it all is the God of history. The people of Israel learned by faith to take all human events seriously in order to know what God was teaching them. This was true individually as well as for the nation.

They learned the importance of faithful response to the outreach of God; they learned that they must be obedient to whatever He commanded or desired.

It is clear that the knowledge of God gained through these experiences was not a static faith floating through a man's consciousness; it was something to be done. Knowledge and truth in the Bible involve things to do, not simply a belief in a God of nature nor an experience of the God within. God is too busy, too active, too dynamic to wait for us to experience him in the acts of worship we devise in our schedules. He is to be known by what he has done and said, by what he is now doing and saying; and he is known when we do what he commands us to do.[1]

Watching the development of this faith in God is the thrilling adventure we have before us as we take a jet flight from Genesis to Revelation. During this growing faith in one God, the people of long ago asked the same questions we ask today: *Who am I? Where did I come from? Where am I going? Why is there evil in the world? Is God real? Why doesn't He make me be good? How can I have relationship with God when I can't see Him? Why are my social relationships important? What about men and women? How responsible am I after all if God made me this way?*

The first eleven chapters of Genesis seek to answer some of these questions. They explain about God and His sovereignty, His power and purpose, His watchful attitude toward the world He made, and His grace and goodness. They affirm man's unique likeness to God, his moral responsibility, his place in God's universe,

26

his sinfulness and its consequences, his necessary struggle with evil, and his hope of victory over it. In fact, these chapters are an introduction to the whole Bible story.

The most important revelation of all is that man can have a relationship with God. This two-sided relationship between God and man did not develop out of any abstract doctrine but from personal experience through the events of life. We can be thankful we have this story of man-and-God relationship. The God of the Bible is a personal God, and He relates to every man in a personal way. Even prayer in the Old Testament is usually described in terms of conversation — God said to man, and man said to God. When God spoke He expected response, and when man spoke he expected an answer. What often sounds anthropomorphic to us was really their way of expressing how personal they knew God to be. Such an understanding of God was entirely unique. Because of their faithfulness to this understanding of God, they lived far above their culture. The main story of the Bible is about the people who were God-conditioned rather than circumstance-conditioned. The prophets had the spiritual insight to see God's will, no matter what social pressures were upon them.

The crown of God's creation was the creation of man and woman. Making them in His own image meant there was a likeness that made communication possible. This does not mean man was created a puppet. From the very beginning Adam and Eve were given the responsibility of choice. To that extent God limited Himself. He has never forced man's choice. This is why the God-man relationship is such a long story. Man is free to disobey God as well as to obey Him.

This freedom was soon misused. The story of Adam and Eve and their temptation is so modern it would be funny if it were not so tragic. God built workable laws into the creation of the world, and He did the same in man. When these laws are obeyed, everything works fine. If they are not obeyed, trouble follows. (You can't break the law of gravity; you only break yourself if you defy that law. However, you can transcend the law of gravity by obeying a higher law.) Eve *listened* to the discrediting of God's laws. The fruit of the forbidden tree looked good, and it was also beautiful. Why shouldn't she be wise and learn by her own experience? She tasted the fruit and liked it, so Adam tasted it too. The consequences were unexpected.

To their surprise the good taste turned to shame. This was indeed a new experience. Then "they heard the sound of the Lord God walking in the garden in the cool of the day," and they tried to hide. This, too, was a new experience. They found no hiding place. So they knew fear for the first time. When they heard the question, "Where are you?" Adam answered, "I heard the sound of thee in the garden, and I was afraid, because I was naked; and I hid myself." Again God asked, "Who told you that you were naked? Have you eaten of the tree of which I commanded you not to eat?" (What a wise counselor God was!) Then, just as people do today, Adam blamed the whole affair on another, his wife, and she in turn blamed it on the tempter (Gen. 3:8-13).

And so sin entered into the world. This first definition of sin was disobedience to God, and the consequence was a break in the relationship with God. And the reason for disobedience was in centering on self rather than on God, an overstepping of human responsibility. So the basic biblical sin is self-centeredness.

The first two children born to this first family were brothers of extremely different dispositions. Even in their worship one was so jealous of the other that he killed him! This was the first religious fight!

Don't let anyone disturb you by asking where Cain got his wife. That is not the point of this story. The point is that man was created to have fellowship wth God, but disobedience interfered with that fellowship.

As generations of people came and went, wickedness predominated. Their wickedness was so great that destruction was inevitable. Only one family was saved from a great flood. The father of this family, Noah, was the only one still in communication with God. Noah listened and was directed to build an ark. People made fun of him, but he did not mind. Then the rains came. Noah, his family, and all the creatures he took with them into the ark were saved.

For this amazing story we really don't need evidence, but if you want it, it certainly is available. Archaeological discoveries in Mesopotamia as well as ancient secular accounts verify the historical fact of a great flood such as was never known before or since.

29

Noah and his family were granted the privilege of man's second chance on earth. Even though Noah had communicated with God, he still was far from perfect. He provided the first record of drunkenness!

Following the story of Noah we are taken through generations of families until we come to Abraham. With Abraham we come to the real beginning of the story of a people chosen by God for the special purpose of carrying the message of God's love and salvation to all who have lost the secret of fellowship with God.

[1]Reginald H. Fuller and G. Ernest Wright, *The Book of the Acts of God* (New York: Doubleday, 1957), p. 22.

3
ABRAHAM,
THE MAN OF FAITH

Hebrew history begins with the story of Abraham. Abraham's claim to this position was his faith in one God, a miracle in his day, for the generations that followed Noah had long since forgotten about one God.

Abraham, the son of Terah, was born in Ur of the Chaldees. Ur was a flourishing city on the Euphrates River. After centuries of affluence Ur disappeared from history, possibly because the great river had changed its course. Was there a city named Ur? It was practically a legend until 1854 when J. E. Taylor, then British consul at Basra, was able after excavations to identify the city as Ur. The main discoveries of this city were made by Sir Leonard Wooley from 1922 to 1934. Whether Terah, with Abraham and the rest of his family, left Ur in its golden age, as Wooley believed, or later has not been determined. In any case, the date of their departure was probably around 2000 B.C.

Ur was a city of idolatry. It was the center for the worship of the moon god, Sin, and fabulous temples have been excavated. The Bible tells us, "Your fathers lived of old beyond the Euphrates, Terah, the father of Abraham and of Nahor; and they served other gods" (Josh. 24:2). According to legends, Terah made idols which he sold in his shop. Other legends tell of Abraham's boyhood. He loved the outdoors, especially at night. From a cave facing east he would often watch the stars fade and the sun rise. He learned the dependability of the sun and stars. The stars probably meant the most to him because God spoke to him later in terms of the stars.

The legendary story I like best is about little Abram, as he was first called. Something must have happened to him as he watched the stars, because he got a sense of worship from watching them which he never felt before the idols his father made. Whenever his father left him to care for the shop, Abram seldom sold anything. Perhaps he spoke to everyone as he did to a woman who came in one day. She wanted an idol to protect her from thieves, as her other idol had been stolen. Abram said, "How do you think another idol can protect you since the last one failed to do so?" Ignoring his remark, the woman chose one she wanted. Abram asked, "How old are you?" The woman said, "Sixty." Abram said, "My father made that idol three weeks ago. How do you think it can protect you?" Then Abram took a big stick and began to break the idols all around the shop. The woman fled in fright. When Abram realized what he was doing, he put the stick in the hand of the largest idol — and awaited the return of his father! His father was shocked at the sight of all the destruction. He said, "Son, what has happened here?" Abram answered, "The big idol got angry and knocked out all the little idols."[1]

Such a legend might easily have had a basis in fact because Abram was ready to hear the voice of God and to respond to that voice in faith. A listening ear has to be trained. When everyone else, including his family, worshiped idols, there must have been a reason for Abram's ability to hear the voice of an unseen God.

If you ever have doubts about God, especially since some theologians have pronounced Him dead, you will know how remarkable it was for Abram to come to such a conviction. How Abram could come to the place where he could have such a faith intrigues me more than anything else about him. Abram didn't pick this up from his culture, and chances are he did not get any help from his home.

In all worship of other gods the virtue and the efficacy of the worship depend on the initiative of the worshiper. How did Abram know he must turn that around — to "hear a voice," and to recognize it as from outside himself, even with such assurance that he could stake his whole future on it? There must have been an unusual quietness in his soul, for we never hear God unless we are quiet.

When Terah left Ur, we do not know whether he was seeking new security or whether he merely had the sense of adventure his son Abram seemed to have. Anyway, he followed the route of other pilgrims and landed in Haran, one thousand miles away, another city of the moon god. Here the family settled, and here Terah died many years later.

It was in Haran that Abram heard the voice of God: "Go from your country and your kindred and your father's house to the land that I will show you" (Gen. 12:1). He also heard the promise that he would be the progenitor of a great nation. At this time Abram was seventy-five years old and had no children. How could he believe such a promise? But he went anyway.

Some modern people have called Abram a hobo, but that term does not give the proper impression of this man at all. He was rich, and he was a family man. True, he did not know where he was going, but he did know whom he followed (Gen. 12:1-9).

He came from a city of advanced civilization. He was not a nomad who raided or claimed squatter's rights. He negotiated leases for land he needed and paid for the right to draw water from wells. He dealt with princes as their peer. Dr. Kelso called him an international businessman and merchant prince.[2]

When Abram came with his caravan to Shechem, the Lord appeared to him and said, "To your descendants I will give this land" (12:7). I don't know how God appeared to him, but I know that Abram knew who spoke to him and what was said. He was so grateful that he built an altar there to worship God. Then he moved on to Bethel and built another altar where he "called upon the name of the Lord." Later a famine came and

34

he and his household went to Egypt to escape it. In Egypt Abram acted according to the custom of the day in regard to his beautiful wife. He acted out of fear, not faith, and got into trouble, so they had to leave Egypt. He returned to Bethel, rich in silver, gold, and cattle (12:10–13:4). Here he worshiped the Lord at the altar he had previously built.

Because of servant troubles Abram had to separate from his nephew, Lot. Again in this time of crisis, the Lord appeared to Abram and renewed the promise that all the land he could see would belong to his descendants. Abram moved his tent and went to dwell by the Oaks of Mamre, where he built another altar to the Lord. (There is a beautiful ancient oak tree still alive in that place. It is propped up and fenced in so tourists will not disturb it.)

All the promises given to Abram for his descendants became a growing test for his faith. Descendants? He and his wife still had no children. Added to this was the fact that childlessness brought the stigma of being in disfavor with God or the gods. Abram had much to think about. Being alone in his faith in one God, it took great courage to hold that faith. But God remembered him.

> *After these things the word of the LORD came to Abram in a vision, "Fear not, Abram, I am your shield; your reward shall be very great." But Abram said, "O Lord GOD, what wilt thou give me, for I continue childless, and the heir of my house is Eliezer of Damascus? . . . Behold thou hast given me no offspring; and a slave born in my*

*house will be my heir." And behold, the word of
the LORD came to him, "This man shall not be
your heir; your own son shall be your heir." And
he brought him outside and said, "Look toward
heaven, and number the stars, if you are able to
number them. . . . So shall your descendants
be." And he believed the LORD; and he reckoned it
to him as righteousness (15:1-6).*

Sarai, Abram's wife, evidently did not have her
own experience of faith, and she had a difficult time
going on her husband's faith, so she decided to work
things out according to the custom of the day. She said
to Abram, "Behold now, the LORD has prevented me
from bearing children; go in to my maid; it may be that I
shall obtain children by her" (16:2). Abram must have
reasoned that such a child would indeed be his own
child, so he did as his wife suggested, and in due time
Ishmael was born.

Thirteen years went by after the birth of Ishmael.
Abram loved the boy very much even though Sarai and
Hagar had a hard time getting along with each other.

Then God appeared to Abram again (17:1–18:15).
There was no doubt in Abram's mind about this communication. God confirmed His covenant with Abram
and all the promises He had given him. Next He
changed Abram's name to Abraham, meaning "the
father of a multitude." Then God added, "Sarai your
wife, you shall not call her name Sarai, but Sarah shall be
her name. I will bless her, and moreover I will give you a
son by her; I will bless her, and she shall be a mother of
nations; kings of peoples shall come from her."

36

Abram, now Abraham, could not help but laugh. He fell on his face and said to *himself,* "Shall a child be born to a man who is a hundred years old? Shall Sarah, who is ninety years old, bear a child?"

Then Abraham said to God, "Oh, that Ishmael might live in thy sight!" God said, "No, but Sarah your wife shall bear you a son, and you shall call his name Isaac." Then the Lord appeared to Abraham by the Oaks of Mamre through three men. The men were entertained royally, and after a sumptuous feast they asked for Sarah. She was eavesdropping at the tent door. When Abraham was told again that Sarah would have a child, Sarah laughed to herself, but the guests knew. And they asked a wonderful question: "Is anything too hard for the Lord?"

Nothing *was* too hard for the Lord. Sarah did bear a son in due time, and Abraham called his name Isaac. Only someone who knows the East can fully appreciate what this meant to Sarah — to have her reproach taken away from her. But now she couldn't stand to have little Isaac playing with her servant's son. *Her* son was now the heir. Sarah's heart became hard toward Hagar and Ishmael, so Abraham sent Hagar and Ishmael away; but he sent them with God's promise for Ishmael's descendants.

The father-son relationship between Abraham and Isaac must have been remarkable. The years of waiting with promises only, the hopes through an adopted son blasted, their contrivance for a son by the servant girl rejected by God — all these seeming disappointments only made the miracle of Isaac the greater. Fathers of that day placed their hopes for the future in the oldest son. Sons in that culture honored their fathers. Abraham was a man to be honored, and Isaac was a well-dispositioned person from all we know of him. Nothing in his life tested his faith so much as the test that was coming to him.

In the culture of Abraham's day, the people who worshiped idols followed a barbarous custom: When they wanted to make the supreme sacrifice to their gods, they would sacrifice the oldest son for whom they held the highest hopes. Abraham saw all this. Did he love his son more than his God? He knew God was asking him this question. Abraham felt he had to prove his faith.

One morning he rose early, took two servants, his beloved son, Isaac, wood, fire, and a knife. They walked and walked. Imagine Abraham's thoughts! On the third day he left the servants with the donkey and told them to wait until he and Isaac returned. Isaac carried the wood and Abraham carried the fire and the knife as they walked up the mountain together. At last Isaac broke the silence, "My father!" Abraham must have known what was coming, but he answered only, "Here am I, my son." Isaac asked the dreaded question, "Behold the fire and the wood; but where is the lamb for the burnt offering?" Abraham could answer only within the area of his faith, "God will provide himself the lamb for a burnt offering, my son." The story says, "So they went both of them together."

If this had been a Canaanite father and son, the father would have been beating his breast and pulling his hair until he would be drugged by suffering, for in his normal mind he would never be able to destroy his firstborn son. Perhaps he would drug his son also; at the least he would be controlled by fear. But Abraham and Isaac walked up the mountain *quietly* together. This is one of the differences between worship of God and other kinds of religious experience. The man who knows God *waits on Him,* but the pagan must take the desperate initiative toward his God.

The obedience of Isaac and his honor for his father are underscored as he let his father put him on the altar and bind him there. Did he not cry out or protest? I don't know. He may have been too shocked to speak. Or did he still have hope that the Lord would intervene? Well, the Lord did. As Abraham lifted his knife to strike his son, a distinct voice called, "Abraham, Abraham!" Abraham answered, "Here am I." What glad words he heard: "Do not lay your hand on the lad or do anything to him; for now I know that you fear God, seeing that you have not withheld your son, your only son, from me." Abraham lifted his eyes and saw a ram in the thicket which he caught and sacrificed instead of his son. Abraham named that place Jehovah-jirah, which means "The Lord will provide." Then the Lord renewed his covenant with Abraham, telling him again of the promises for him and his descendants. So Abraham and Isaac went back to the servants waiting on the mountainside, and together they all returned to Beersheba.

Abraham had one more responsibility toward his son. Isaac was twenty-seven years old when his mother died, and Abraham was concerned about the kind of wife Isaac should have. He did not want Isaac to get involved with any of the idol-worshiping Canaanite girls among whom they lived. So Abraham called his trusted servant, who had charge of all his house, and sent him back to Haran to find a wife for Isaac from among Abraham's relatives there. If you want to read a delightful love story, read Genesis 24. This servant also trusted God, and he was led to the right girl for Isaac. When she came back with the servant, Isaac loved her at once and was comforted at the loss of his mother.

No other man of Abraham's day had faith like his. God reached through to Abraham in a culture alien to his faith. It is one of the great miracles of religious history that Abraham responded and that he continued in that faith in spite of all other social pressures. Centuries later Paul could say, "Abraham believed God, and it was reckoned to him as righteousness. . . . he grew strong in faith as he gave glory to God, fully convinced that God was able to do what he had promised" (Rom. 4:3,20,21).

In Abraham a pattern of relationship was set: Abraham was called by God; a covenant or relationship was established; Abraham then was given a commission to be a blessing to others.

No man is called to a relationship with God just for his own benefit; he is always called to enter into God's concern for all others who do not know Him.

[1]Joseph Gaer, *The Lore of the Old Testament,* pp. 86, 87.
[2]James Kelso, *Archaeology and Our Old Testament Contemporaries,* pp. 16, 18.

4
MOSES, *A* CHOSEN MAN AND *A* CHOSEN NATION

Abraham's faith was not only a personal faith but a covenant faith. God came to him not only for a personal relationship but for a ministry to all peoples. God had said to him, "I will make of you a great nation," and "I will bless you, and make your name great, so that you will be a blessing . . . by you all the families of the earth shall bless themselves" (Gen. 12:1-3). But for many long years after Abraham's death, it looked as if this covenant would never be fulfilled. He had been promised a land of his own, but his descendants continued to be a wandering people.

The covenant with Abraham was renewed with Isaac, his son, (Gen. 26:2-5), then with Jacob (Gen. 28:10-17). Then follows the dramatic story of Joseph and the move to Egypt where eventually the Israelites became a great nation, but in slavery. It now looked as if the covenant with Abraham had been forgotten. But the God who cares had not forgotten His covenant with the man who listened in faith, and He waited for a man who would listen again.

By the grace of God a man was prepared. Into the midst of a doomed people a baby was born. The midwife disregarded Pharaoh's command to destroy all Israelite baby boys, and the baby's mother watched over him with great care and ingenuity. The story of his adoption by Pharaoh's daughter is familiar. The miracle of his mother's becoming his nurse for the first years of his life fits the pattern for his preparation. How she must have treasured the privilege of teaching him about the faith of his people and helping him to have a concern for them! He was later educated as an Egyptian prince with all the privileges of the royal household. The princess called him Moses.

One day when Moses was grown, he went out and saw the burdens of his people. An Egyptian was beating one of the Hebrew slaves. Moses could not stand to see this cruel treatment of his people, so he knocked the Egyptian down and accidentally killed him. He hid the body in the sand. When he went out the next day, he saw two Hebrews fighting with each other, so Moses said to the man who was in the wrong, "Why do you strike your fellow?" The man answered, "Who made you a prince and a judge over us? Do you mean to kill me as you killed the Egyptian?" Then Moses was afraid and thought, "Surely the thing is known." When Pharaoh heard of it, he sought to kill Moses.

Moses fled into the desert and must have encountered many dangers for which his sheltered, princely life had not prepared him. When he reached the rugged country of Midian, he sat down by a well. Then seven young women came to draw water for their father's sheep. Suddenly some rough shepherds chased the girls away and used the water for their own flocks. This injustice outraged Moses, so he helped the girls and saw them safely home. Their father was Reuel, or Jethro, a priest. Moses was accepted into Jethro's family and later married one of the daughters. The years Moses spent in this wilderness caring for Jethro's flocks were preparation for the mission God called him to later, but he did not know that he was being prepared for a great task.

The desert provided much silence, the kind that makes or breaks a man. It strengthened Moses. It takes strength to listen to silence and Moses must have learned the art well. One day while tending the flocks,

> he led his flock to the west side of the wilderness, and came to Horeb, the mountain of God. And the angel of the LORD appeared to him in a flame of fire out of the midst of a bush; and he looked, and lo, the bush was burning, yet it was not consumed. And Moses said, "I will turn aside and see this great sight, why the bush is not burnt." When the LORD saw that he turned aside to see, God called to him out of the bush, "Moses, Moses!" And he said, "Here am I." Then he said, "Do not come near; put off your shoes from your feet, for the place on which you are standing is holy ground." And he said, "I am the God of your father, the God of Abraham, the God of Isaac,

43

and the God of Jacob." And Moses hid his face,
for he was afraid to look at God (Exod. 3:1-6).

If this experience had ended there, Moses would have
had a wonderful "testimony" to give of his experience
of God; but the God of the Bible does not stop there
when he comes to man. He comes to enlist the called
man in a cooperative effort in His concern for the
people He loves.

So the Lord said to Moses,

I have seen the affliction of my people who are in
Egypt, and have heard their cry because of their
taskmasters; I know their sufferings, and I have
come down to deliver them out of the hand of the
Egyptians, and to bring them up out of that land to
a good and broad land. . . . And now, behold, the
cry of the people of Israel has come to me, and I
have seen the oppression with which the Egyp-
tians oppress them. Come, I will send you to
Pharaoh that you may bring forth my people, the
sons of Israel, out of Egypt (Exod. 3:7-10).

That's the pattern of cooperation between God and
man!

Moses was reluctant to go because he was conscious of his inadequacy. Why would Pharaoh listen to
him? God told him the Pharaoh who had sought his life
was dead, and He would be with him to meet the new
Pharaoh. But would the people of Israel listen to him
even though he told them the God of their fathers had
sent him? What if they asked, "What is his name?"
And God said to Moses, "Say this to the people of
Israel, 'I AM has sent me to you' " (3:13,14).

The last hesitancy of Moses was because of his slow speech. Then the Lord said to him, "Who has made man's mouth? . . . Is it not I?" The Lord met him in this weakness and sent his brother Aaron with him. So Moses took his family, with the blessing of his father-in-law, and met his brother Aaron at the mountain where God had told him to go. Moses told Aaron all that had happened to him, and together they gathered all the elders of the people of Israel.

> And Aaron spoke all the words which the LORD had spoken to Moses, and did the signs in the sight of the people. And the people believed; and when they heard that the LORD had visited the people of Israel and that he had seen their affliction, they bowed their heads and worshiped (4:30,31).

It is interesting to note that when Moses became involved in the responsibility of leadership, he soon did his own talking instead of waiting for his brother to speak for him. When he forgot himself, he was free to speak of God.

After winning the support of the Hebrews, a slave people, Moses and Aaron faced the most formidable enemy — the whole Egyptian system of worldly, oppressive power. Could the Lord of Israel be stronger? They started with the faith that their God was stronger. This faith got a little shaky when the way got hard, but at least in such moments of discouragement Moses turned to the Lord, and each time he received assurance in the way God directed him.

It was a different story with the people. At each point of discouragement they murmured against Moses and questioned the faithfulness of God. When they finally did get away from Pharaoh and thought they were on the way to freedom, the greatest test came. Pharaoh changed his mind again and pursued them. How could he let these slaves go?

> When Pharaoh drew near, the people of Israel lifted up their eyes, and behold the Egyptians were marching after them; and they were in great fear. And the people of Israel cried out to the LORD; and they said to Moses, "Is it because there are no graves in Egypt that you have taken us away to die in the wilderness? What have you done to us, in bringing us out of Egypt? Is not this what we said to you in Egypt, 'Let us alone and let us serve the Egyptians'? For it would have been better for us to serve the Egyptians than to die in the wilderness (14:10-12).

Moses answered the people with a most daring statement of faith:

> Fear not, stand firm, and see the salvation of the LORD, which he will work for you today; for the Egyptians whom you see today, you shall never see again. The LORD will fight for you, and you have only to be still (14:13,14).

So Moses stretched out his hand, the waters parted, the Hebrews were saved, and the pursuers were destroyed.

In the years to come, part of the Hebrew liturgy of worship was praise for this deliverance (Deut. 26: 5-11).

Although freed from the Egyptians, the Hebrews' troubles did not end. Many times Moses must have felt they had just begun. A slave people afraid of freedom, they often longed for the security of slavery! They were not ready to meet the enemies in the land to which they were going. They needed to be forged into a nation. They needed inner discipline. They needed a wilderness experience as Moses had needed it, but they didn't like it. Nevertheless, the people were brought to an experience of a definite religious faith, a definite law, and a definite worship. A group of rebellious slaves was forged into a covenant people under God, the God of Abraham, Isaac, and Jacob.

They were told, "I am the LORD your God, who brought you out of the land of Egypt, out of the house of bondage. You shall have no other gods before me" (Exod. 20:2,3). But the people were slow to learn. They wanted the security of something visible.

When Moses went up on Mount Sinai, the people took things into their own hands. They "gathered around Aaron, saying, 'Come on, make us some god to go in front of us; as for this Moses, the man who brought us out of the land of Egypt, we don't know what has become of him!' " This suggestion came from the spokesman of a people who had no vision and were easily discouraged.

Aaron knew what Moses knew; he should have had better sense and better spiritual understanding than the people. But,

> *Aaron said to them, "Break off the golden earrings from the ears of your wives and sons and daughters, and bring them to me." So the people all broke off their earrings and handed them to*

Aaron, who took and carved them with a tool into a metal calf. The people cried, "Here is your God, O Israel, who brought you out of the land of Egypt!" At this, Aaron erected an altar in front of the calf and proclaimed a festival the next day for the Eternal. [1] [What a compromise for a supposed leader!] *So the next morning the people arose and offered burnt-offerings, and brought recompense-offerings; then the people sat down to the sacrificial feast, after which they rose to amuse themselves (Exod. 32:1-6 Moffatt).*

This is the evidence of false worship; it is self-centeredness!

Moses came down from the mountain in great despair when he saw what had happened. He asked Aaron, "What did this people do to you, that you let them incur great guilt?" Then Aaron answered,

Let not my lord's [his brother's] *anger blaze; you know how determined the people are to do wrong. They told me to make gods for them, to go in front of them, crying, "As for this Moses, the man who brought us out of the land of Egypt, we don't know what has become of him!" I told them to break off any gold they possessed, and they gave it to me; I just threw it into the fire and out came this calf! (vv. 21-24 Moffatt).*

But Moses was a "man of God leader"! How he had grown spiritually! The next day Moses told the people he would return to the mountain alone with God, and he would pray for them. And what a prayer! "Ah, this people has committed a great sin, making a golden god for themselves! Yet, wilt thou not forgive their sin? If thou wilt not, then pray blot me out of thy list of the living" (vv. 31,32 *Moffatt*). The Lord practically told Moses that forgiveness and punishment were his prerogative; "However, go and lead the people where I have told you, and my angel shall go in front of you" (v. 34 *Moffatt*). Even though the people had failed God and Moses, Moses still could love them, and God did too.

The central event of the forty years wandering in the wilderness was the giving of the Ten Commandments which Moses brought down with him from Mount Sinai. The law which Moses gave the people from God was unique and entirely new because it was God-centered law, and it came with a covenant. "If you will obey my voice and keep my covenant, you shall be my own possession among all peoples; for all the earth is mine, and you shall be to me a kingdom of priests and a holy nation." And all the people answered, "All that the LORD has spoken we will do."

Moses died at the gate of the Promised Land, but he left behind him a real monument: a people set for freedom, a new law from God, and a covenant with his people. He left the memory of a great leader called of God to be used as a turning point in history. God's revelation of Himself to Moses and the people is still revelation to us.

---

[1] I understand that before Dr. Moffatt died he said he would translate it "the Lord" instead of "the Eternal" if he had it to do over.

5
SAMUEL, JUDGE AND PROPHET

Just when we feel overwhelmed by the spiritual understanding of Moses, we have to face the fact that he was not permitted to enter the land of promise. But he accepted God's reproof most graciously (Deut. 32:48-52). Erich Fromm said of this, "The prophet who even for a moment puts himself in the center shows that he is not ready to be a leader *in* freedom, but only *to* freedom."[1]

Joshua was appointed by God and blessed by Moses to be the new leader of the people. God asked Joshua to keep the covenant and to keep up his courage. The people seemed to do well under Joshua's leadership, but after him, in the period of the judges, it was another story.

This period of adjustment in the new land, as recorded in the Book of Judges, is a sad tale of a vicious cycle repeated many times: idolatry, punishment by an oppressor, repentance, and then salvation through a leader whom God raised up. One wonders how God could have had such patience with a people whom He had chosen, a people who repeatedly failed in their part of the covenant with Him. So easily they forgot about the one God and succumbed to the worship of Baal and other gods, even to the practice of human sacrifice and sex orgies.

As I read again through the Book of Judges, the periods of repentance and deliverance were a respite, but the relief didn't last long. The influence of their idolatrous neighbors was stronger than their faith in one God. One has to wonder which is worse — the sex-oriented culture of today with sex as an end in itself, or their sex-oriented culture in the name of their gods.

As I had to think to myself, if only this immature and evil part of the story of God's people had not been told. How could this story be "inspired"? For it is only when the people lived above their culture that they could be counted truly as people of God. Only that part of the Old Testament lived above the culture line is background for the New Testament.

Then I remembered that the Bible is the story of *God* — the God who created man and limited Himself by giving man the freedom of choice. He is a God who *waits* for man to learn his lessons until he can choose God with his whole heart. For the first time I fully realized how all these terrible stories can be part of God's inspired Word. They were inspired to be written, not to be imitated or defended; they were to show man's

51

responsibility of choosing right from wrong. This is why Jesus most truly revealed the Father on the cross. Now as I read the unhappy parts of the story of God's chosen people, I feel a new surrounding of the boundless love of God.

It also helps to understand the patience of God when we see the transition through which the children of Israel were passing. Jehovah God had come to them through the leadership of Moses and Joshua, as a God revealed in dramatic events of history. Now they were settling down to a completely new way of living. They were no longer wanderers but agriculturists. They were now dependent upon the cycles of nature for success in their crops, and it was easy to look to their Canaanite neighbors, who were experienced farmers.

It is not surprising, then, that the Israelites turned to the gods of the land. The divine powers of these gods were revealed in the mystery of fertility. Sex for the Canaanites was elevated to the realm of the divine. By ritually imitating the action of god and goddess, they believed they could assist the fertility powers through magic. Through sexual ceremonies farmers thought they could swing into the rhythms of the agricultural world! (See Deut. 23:17,18.) The Canaanites thought that to have good crops they had to manipulate their gods by being partakers in religious prostitution. So the Israelites, new to agriculture, turned to the nature religion of their neighbors until they were faced with another crisis. Then they would turn again to their God, who revealed Himself in events of history. It took them a long time to learn that their God was an all-purpose

God and would have no other gods before Him.

God was waiting.

The last judge of this period of tribal confederacy was Samuel. His ministry marked the transition between the old charismatic leadership and the new prophetic leadership, which from this time on was to be the style of spiritual leadership in Israel. "The word of the LORD was rare in those days; there was no frequent vision" (1 Sam. 3:1). But now new hope dawned.

In the midst of Israel there were some who remained faithful to their God. There were Elkanah and his wife Hannah. Elkanah had taken a second wife because Hannah proved barren. After she had children, the second wife deliberately irritated Hannah, but Hannah remained the favorite wife. Elkanah loved her deeply. One day he said to her, "Hannah, why do you weep? And why do you not eat? And why is your heart sad? Am I not more to you than ten sons?" (1 Sam. 1:8). Her husband's love was not enough for Hannah; she wanted a son.

While they were at Shiloh for worship, Hannah prayed with all her heart for a son and promised to give him in service to God. In due time Samuel was born. What joy this brought to Hannah! God had heard her prayer, and she did not forget her promise to the Lord. When Samuel was but a little boy, she brought him to Eli, the priest, and said,

> *Oh, my lord! As you live, my lord, I am the woman who was standing here in your presence, praying to the LORD. For this child I prayed; and the LORD has granted me my petition which I made to him.*

53

Therefore I have lent him to the LORD; as long as he lives, he is lent to the LORD (1:26-28).

So Samuel stayed with Eli in the house of the Lord and helped in the care of the sanctuary.

Then one night Samuel heard his name called. He went to Eli, but Eli had not called him. When this happened the third time, Eli perceived that the Lord was speaking to Samuel, so he told Samuel how to answer if the call was repeated. Again the call came, and this time Samuel answered, "Speak, for thy servant hears." The message was an unhappy one and Samuel did not want to tell Eli, but he was obedient and repeated all of the sad message.

And Samuel grew, and the LORD was with him and let none of his words fall to the ground. And all Israel from Dan to Beer-sheba knew that Samuel was established as a prophet of the LORD. And the LORD appeared again at Shiloh, for the LORD revealed himself to Samuel at Shiloh by the word of the LORD (3:19-21).

Samuel judged Israel all the days of his life. When he was old, he appointed his sons to be judges, but they were not men of God — they "turned aside after gain; they took bribes and perverted justice" (8:3).

Then the elders of Israel came to Samuel and said, "Behold, you are old and your sons do not walk in your ways; now appoint for us a king to govern us like all the nations" (8:5). This was hard for Samuel to accept, but the Lord told him that the people were really rejecting God as their king. The Lord told him to listen to the people but to warn them what it would mean to have a king who would command them and tax them. He was to tell the people, "In that day you will cry out because of your king, whom you have chosen for yourselves; but the LORD will not answer you in that day" (8:18). Again God was letting the people take the responsibility for a choice that He was setting them free to make. He was giving them time to learn the lesson they needed to learn.

One day after this call for a king, the Lord said to Samuel,

> *Tomorrow about this time I will send to you a man from the land of Benjamin, and you shall anoint him to be prince over my people Israel. He shall save my people from the hand of the Philistines; for I have seen the affliction of my people, because their cry has come to me (9:16).*

Saul came, hoping that the prophet could tell him where his father's lost donkeys were to be found. Instead of that he found a kingdom! Saul was overcome with surprise; but after the anointing and a religious experience with a band of prophets, he accepted the commission to become king.

Saul was really to be a constitutional monarch, while Samuel continued to be the spiritual guide for him and for the people. After Saul had begun his reign, Samuel called the people to Gilgal to renew the kingdom under God. Those who had not yet accepted Saul as king accepted him that day. Then Samuel made a farewell speech to the people:

55

*And now, behold, the king walks before you; and I
am old and gray . . . I have walked before you
from my youth until this day. Here I am; testify
against me before the LORD. . . . [He asked if they
had anything against him but no one did.] Now
therefore stand still, that I may plead with you
before the LORD concerning all the saving deeds of
the LORD which he performed for you and for your
fathers. . . . do not turn aside from following the
LORD, but serve the LORD with all your heart; and
do not turn aside after vain things which cannot
profit or save, for they are vain. For the LORD will
not cast away his people, for his great name's
sake, because it has pleased the LORD to make you
a people for himself. Moreover as for me, far be it
from me that I should sin against the LORD by
ceasing to pray for you; and I will instruct you in
the good and the right way. Only fear the LORD,
and serve him faithfully with all your heart; for
consider what great things he has done for you.
But if you still do wickedly, you shall be swept
away, both you and your king (12:2,3,7,20-25).*

In the beginning of his ministry Saul was
seemingly quite humble, but perhaps it was only a
self-consciousness; because after he had won many
victories for the Israelites and had gained much power,
he could not wait for Samuel, his spiritual guide. He did
what many have done before and since who depend on a
call and a religious experience rather than on continual
guidance from the Lord. One day Saul took over a
priest's place in offering sacrifices, and Samuel, with
great spiritual discernment, said to him:

*Has the LORD as great delight in burnt offerings
and sacrifices, as in obeying the voice of the
LORD? Behold, to obey is better than sacrifice,
and to hearken than the fat of rams. For rebellion
is as the sin of divination, and stubbornness is as
iniquity and idolatry. Because you have rejected
the word of the LORD, he has also rejected you
from being king (15:22,23).*

Samuel grieved greatly over Saul. So one day the
Lord said to Samuel,

*How long will you grieve over Saul, seeing I have
rejected him from being king over Israel? Fill
your horn with oil, and go; I will send you to Jesse
the Bethlehemite, for I have provided for myself a
king among his sons (16:1).*

Samuel went to Jesse's house. When he saw the
oldest son, he thought, "Surely, the LORD's anointed is
before him" (16:6). (Perhaps Samuel had the image of
a tall, handsome man like Saul.) But the Lord said to
Samuel, "Do not look on his appearance or on the
height of his stature, because I have rejected him; for
the LORD sees not as man sees; man looks on the
outward appearance, but the LORD looks on the heart"
(16:7).

Seven of Jesse's sons came before Samuel, one
after the other, and Samuel had to admit that God had
chosen none of these. Samuel asked Jesse, "Are all
your sons here?" Jesse answered, "There remains yet
the youngest, but behold, he is keeping the sheep."
Samuel said they could not sit down until he came.
David came, and "he was ruddy, and had beautiful

eyes, and was handsome. And the LORD said, 'Arise, anoint him; for this is he.' '' So Samuel anointed David before his brothers and the ''Spirit of the LORD came mightily upon David from that day forward'' (16:11-13). Now Samuel's hopes lay upon this man chosen by God.

Before David became king, Samuel died. All Israel mourned for him (25:1). They had more reason to mourn than they knew. Only the perspective of history could see the uniqueness of Samuel's ministry. He grew up in the Lord and came into the responsibility of leadership when the people were only a weak confederacy and when their faith in God was weaker still, Samuel brought them together and back to a greater faith in the God of their fathers, but he was disappointed when they rejected the direct kingship of God. They wanted to be like other nations politically, so they asked for a king.

Samuel helped to initiate a new type of monarchy. The king was only to administer the law, the basic freedoms of the people were to be protected against the encroachments of royal power. In the years to come the prophets of Israel continued to have a freedom of speech impossible in any other nation. This was a people chosen by God from the day of Abraham to be a covenant people, with a commission for all peoples. Samuel knew that only as they accepted this responsibility could they hope for success as a nation, for they were to be a *nation under God*.

[1]Erich Fromm, *You Shall Be As Gods* (New York: Holt, Rinehart & Winston, 1966), p. 90.

6
DAVID, KING UNDER GOD

A Sunday school teacher once asked me some simple questions about David. I asked, "Haven't you read the Bible story about him?" She answered, "No, I didn't need to because I saw the movie *David and Bathsheba* last week." I said, "You can't go by that. It was censored!" One of the unique things about the Bible is that it does not censor the stories about its heroes. Remember always that God is the real hero of the Bible.

In David's time the kings of other nations had the right to take any woman they desired without apology or any sense of guilt. David's story contained plenty for Hollywood to feature, but this was only the phase of David's life in which he acted like a man *of his own time and culture*. Kingdom-of-God ethics were not yet clearly defined. The Bible story is really about David *as he lived above his culture.* David was Israel's greatest king because he never forgot that he was a *king under God.* His sins and weaknesses were never minimized, but we marvel at his devotion to God and his humble responsiveness whenever he was checked by God.

David was secretly anointed as God's choice to be king after Saul's failure, but David had to gain the throne the hard way, and it was a long journey from the shepherd's field to the throne. One has to wonder at David's patience during those waiting years. Did the quiet years out in the fields build a deep quietness into his otherwise stormy soul?

David, the shepherd musician, was sought out and brought to court to provide music to soothe King Saul when he was mentally disturbed. Then David came to national attention when he dared to challenge Goliath, the giant of the Philistines. The warrior Goliath disdained this youth who came to him unarmed. But David was fearless because he was there to defend his God: "That all this assembly may know that the LORD saves not with sword and spear; for the battle is the LORD'S and he will give you into our hand" (1 Sam. 17:47).

King Saul honored David until he became jealous of his popularity with the people. In fact, Saul became so violent that David had to flee for his life. He became a leader of a group of outlaws. As King Saul sought his life, twice David had the opportunity to kill him, but David would not lift a hand against the "Lord's anointed."

David's great respect for Saul because he had been

anointed by God was revealed in his patience toward Saul in the midst of his relentless persecution, but even more in his grief at Saul's death. Of course part of that grief was for the loss of Saul's son Jonathan, whom David loved as a brother. But when David heard of the ones who buried Saul, he sent messengers to them, saying, "May you be blessed by the LORD, because you showed this loyalty to Saul your lord, and buried him! Now may the LORD show steadfast love and faithfulness to you! And I will do good to you because you have done this thing" (2 Sam. 2:5,6). No other king of that day (or this) would have acted thus toward an enemy.

When David was free to take the responsibility for which God had anointed him, he did not rush in but continued to wait on the Lord. After the death of Saul, "David inquired of the LORD, 'Shall I go up into any of the cities of Judah?' And the LORD said to him, 'Go up.' David said, 'To which shall I go up?' And he said, 'To Hebron.' So David went up there" (2 Sam. 2:1,2).

At Hebron David reigned over Judah seven years and six months, and he reigned over all Israel and Judah thirty-three years. After David was anointed to be king over Israel also, he needed a central and neutral capital. He finally succeeded in capturing the Jebusite fortress, Jerusalem, and made it his capital. He rebuilt it, strengthened its fortifications, and moved his court there. Later he brought the ark of the covenant there so that Jerusalem would also be the religious center for his people. David called it the city of David. "And David became greater and greater, for the LORD, the God of hosts, was with him" (5:10).

The presence of the ark meant that David's nation was a people of the covenant. He held unswervingly to the sovereignty of God over him and his people. Only through the unconditional submission of the king to God could the people be counted as the people of God, for the king represented the sovereignty of God to them. David knew this well.

David's achievements were remarkable. He forged an empire that ranged from Sinai and the Gulf of Aqaba to southern Syria. For one generation within the reigns of David and Solomon, Israel was the strongest power between the Nile and the Euphrates. Where David's kingship was concerned, he was able to live by faith; but when it came to his private life, he was in a measure a man of his day and his culture.

To Hollywood's financial gain but to the Christian's sorrow, David's greatest failure was in his relationship with Bathsheba. We must first remember that in that day there was yet no social conscience on the matter of polygamy. Besides that, it was the "king's right" to have any woman he desired. The strange thing is not that David took Bathsheba or had her husband killed, but that *he could feel any guilt on the matter!* God's prophet Nathan was there to check the king when he did not wait on the Lord, and Nathan's discernment was indeed far above the culture of that day. And only in Israel would a prophet have the courage to repove a king. Only a king who put God first in his life would accept reproof from any of his subjects, even from a prophet.

Nathan believed David to be a just man. So he

came to him with the parable of the rich man who stole the poor man's ewe lamb to feed his guest instead of killing one from his own large flock. At once David said the lamb must be restored fourfold and the rich man must be put to death. Then Nathan said simply, "Thou art the man!" All David could say was: "I have sinned against the LORD" (12:13). Nathan forgave David in the name of the Lord and did so without preaching a sermon.

The child born to Bathsheba fell ill, and David wrestled with God in prayer for seven days of the child's illness. The servants were afraid to tell him when the baby died, but to their surprise he accepted it as justice and grieved no longer. *He accepted the forgiveness of God* — a spiritual experience that is even more remarkable than the consciousness of guilt. Whether Psalm 51 was written by David or only ascribed to him makes little difference; it is exactly what he experienced and what the collectors of the Psalms recognized as his experience.

When David was old, and his spoiled, handsome son Absalom almost took the kingdom away from him, David had to flee from Jerusalem. The priests and Levites came along bringing the ark of God, but David said to them, "Carry the ark of God back into the city. If I find favor in the eyes of the LORD, he will bring me back and let me see both it and his habitation; but if he says, 'I have no pleasure in you,' behold, here I am, let him do to me what seems good to him" (2 Sam. 15:25,26). Even when seemingly rejected by his family and his subjects, David had no rebellion in his heart against God. And when he heard the sad story of his son's death, he was deeply moved, and he wept: "O my son Absalom, my son, my son Absalom! Would I had died instead of you, O Absalom, my son, my son!" (18:33).

When David knew he was on his deathbed, he had his son Solomon anointed as his successor with the blessing of the prophet Nathan and the priests. In his charge to Solomon, David said:

> *My son, I had it in my heart to build a house to the name of the LORD my God. But the word of the LORD came to me, saying, "You have shed much blood and have waged great wars; you shall not build a house to my name, because you have shed so much blood upon the earth. Behold a son shall be born to you; he shall be a man of peace. I will give him peace from all his enemies round about; for his name shall be Solomon, and I will give peace and quiet to Israel in his days. He shall build a house for my name (1 Chron. 22:7-10).*

David had thought of God as a God of war, so it was far beyond the spiritual discernment of his day, or his historian's day, to think of the shedding of blood as defiling one's hands. *But* David did see that a man of war was not worthy to build the house of God. He certainly did not get this insight from the culture of his day! It came out of his relationship to God.

7
ELIJAH, WHO
STOOD BEFORE GOD

As the years and centuries passed, David became in memory Israel's ideal king — always faithful to God. Israel remembered his reign as one in which the poor and oppressed were protected and justice flourished. Common people felt close to King David, whereas they felt awed and insignificant before the power and glory of Solomon's reign. With Solomon, Israel entered a literary period, a stage of culture never known before. Solomon had international fame and connections, often accomplished by marrying into the royal families of other nations. In fact, accepting a princess to be his wife was part of his peace pacts! (Could seven hundred wives and three hundred concubines be called the life of peace?) Many of these princesses brought their own religions with them, and Solomon catered to them and even worshiped with them. Solomon was also a great builder. His expenditures were tremendous, and the nation had to bear a tax burden for all this glory.

The people may have been proud of the fame of their king, but when Solomon died, they remembered only the burden of the high taxes they had to pay. So the ten northern tribes separated themselves into another nation. From this time on, Israel's history as a people of the covenant was told not by her rulers but by the prophets sent by God to be the keepers of the conscience of the people. One king after another, so far as Israel's history was concerned, was recorded as practically incidental to the work of a prophet.

After several years the throne of the northern kingdom was seized by Omri, who was a great ruler according to secular history. Even in Assyrian records his kingdom was known as the "house of Omri." He made marriage alliances with surrounding nations as Solomon had done. He had his son Ahab married to a Sidonian princess, Jezebel, who was also a priestess of Baal. When Ahab became king, the Baal priestess became queen. I suppose contemporary appraisal would say she brought culture to Israel, but religious history says she brought idolatry. Ahab built a temple for her in Samaria, his capital, fully equipped for idol worship. Jezebel was a passionate woman and a fanatic in her devotion to her gods. It is said that she imported 850 of her pagan prophets and supported them out of the public treasury. She also set up a campaign to get rid of the prophets of God.

We remember that Baal was a fertility god, so the

rain needed for the farmers' crops was in his realm of power. It was at this juncture that Elijah suddenly appeared. He came into cultured Israel wearing a garment of haircloth and a leather girdle (2 Kings 1:8). He announced to King Ahab, "As the LORD the God of Israel lives, before whom I stand, there shall be neither dew nor rain these years, except by my word" (1 Kings 17:1). Then Elijah disappeared as suddenly as he had come. He hid himself east of Jordan until the streams went dry, and then the Lord sent him to dwell in Jezebel's territory in the home of a widow to whom he became a great blessing.

In the third year of the drought the Lord said to Elijah, "Go, show yourself to Ahab; and I will send rain upon the earth" (1 Kings 18:1). Evidently Elijah did not hesitate to go at the Lord's command even though Ahab had sought everywhere in order to kill him. While on his way to Ahab, Elijah met Obadiah, a friend of God's prophets, whom Ahab had sent out to find water and grass to save his cattle. Obadiah exclaimed, "Is it you, my lord Elijah?" And Elijah answered, "It is I. Go, tell your lord, 'Behold, Elijah is here.'" Obadiah was deeply frightened; he knew his life was at stake if he reported Elijah's presence and Elijah failed to appear. Finally, with Elijah's promise, Obadiah was willing to risk it. He reported to Ahab, and Ahab went to meet Elijah. When he saw Elijah, he said, "Is it you, you troubler of Israel?" Elijah answered, "I have not troubled Israel; but you have, and your father's house, because you have forsaken the commandments of the LORD and followed the Baals."

Then Elijah suggested that they have a contest on Mount Carmel between Baal and Jehovah. Elijah alone would stand in for Jehovah and 450 prophets of Baal would stand in for their gods (18:7-19).

Hosts of people came to see the contest. Elijah said to the people, "How long will you go limping with two different opinions? If the LORD is God, follow him; but if Baal, then follow him." The people waited. Elijah continued, "I, even I only, am left a prophet of the LORD; but Baal's prophets are four hundred and fifty men." Elijah had stated that whichever god answered by sending fire for the altars would be the real God (18:21-24).

Elijah told the prophets of Baal to go first. They prepared their altar and had first choice of a bull for their sacrifice. They called on their god from morning until noon, crying, "O Baal, answer us!" They danced frantically around the altar they had made, but nothing happened. Elijah mocked them: "Cry aloud, for he is a god; either he is musing, or he has gone aside, or he is on a journey, or perhaps he is asleep and must be awakened." So the Baal priests "cried aloud, and cut themselves after their custom with swords and lances, until the blood gushed out upon them. . . . They raved on until the time of the offering of the oblation, but there was no voice; no one answered, no one heeded" (18:28,29). No rain came. The prophets of Baal had to admit defeat.

Then Elijah called all the people to come near him. He prepared his altar, the wood, the sacrifice, and, strangest of all, he had the people fill up the trench three times with water and had them soak everything thoroughly. Then Elijah prayed, "O LORD, God of Abraham, Isaac, and Israel, let it be known this day that thou art God in Israel, and that I am thy servant, and that I have done all these things at thy word. Answer me, O LORD, answer me, that this people may know that thou, O LORD, art God, and that thou hast turned their hearts back" (vv. 36,37). Then the fire of the Lord fell and consumed everything, including the stones and the water! When the people saw this, they fell on their faces and cried out, "The LORD, he is God; the LORD, he is God." So the victory was won for the Lord, the God of Israel.

Then Elijah told Ahab to hurry home because the rains were coming. The drought was over.

The great contrast on Mount Carmel was not between one prophet of God in a contest with hundreds of Baal prophets, nor was it between the different ways of preparing the altars; the contrast was between pagan religion in prayer and a man of God in prayer. The pagan prophets had to mutilate themselves and use all their energies to beg their god to hear them. *All the initiative and effort was on their part*. But the man of God was only responding to his God, and *in quietness and faith* he prayed and waited for God to hear. The real God did hear, and the fire came.

The incident at the foot of the mountain after this great victory was a completely different story. Here Elijah did not wait on his God. *All his quietness was gone*. It is true he was a courageous man of action, but on the mountain that was tempered by his *waiting* on

69

the Lord. Now he was a "fire-breathing activist." The victory for the Lord wasn't enough for Elijah; he wanted victory *over* the priests of Baal as well. His culture had taken over. From their hours of self-immolation the priests of Baal were greatly weakened, and they had no strength left to defend themselves. Elijah ordered the people to seize the helpless men. Then Elijah brought them down to the Brook Kishon and killed them. To put it mildly, that was quite a bloody ordeal! Human nature being what it is — now as well as then — there wasn't much left of Elijah's consciousness of a holy God who had heard his prayer on top of the mount.

When Ahab told Jezebel what Elijah had done to her prophet-priests, she was furious. She sent a messenger to Elijah, saying, "So may the gods do to me, and more also, if I do not make your life as the life of one of them by this time tomorrow." Then Elijah was afraid, and he fled (1 Kings 19).

Throughout my young life this story bothered me. Why should fearless Elijah suddenly be afraid of a woman — even Jezebel? I was never satisfied until I saw what had happened to Elijah spiritually. Any man so sensitive to God's Spirit that he could go through the pregnant quietness of his faith in God up on the mount would naturally be disturbed by the gruesome experience of murder immediately following, whether he had a "reasonable theological explanation" or not. This was truly a letdown in faith, even though we *cannot* blame him because of spiritual truths he had still not perceived. (Jesus had not come yet!) Now I am sure

Elijah did not run from Jezebel; *he tried to run from himself*.

After weeks of hiding in the wilderness cave on Mount Horeb, the word of the Lord came to Elijah again: "What are you doing here, Elijah?" Elijah was still full of self-pity and self-defense. He answered the Lord, "I have been very jealous for the LORD, the God of hosts; for the people of Israel have forsaken thy covenant, thrown down thy altars, and slain thy prophets with the sword; and I, even I only, am left; and they seek my life to take it away" (19:10). Had Elijah forgotten the victory for the Lord on Mount Carmel and the response of the people to that victory? He had not yet faced what *he* had done; he remembered only what Jezebel had done. Then the Lord said to him, "Go forth, stand upon the mount before the LORD." Elijah was now in an attitude whereby he could come back to God-consciousness and out of self-defeat.

Elijah waited.

A great and strong wind rent the mountains, and broke in pieces the rocks before the LORD, but the LORD was not in the wind; *and after the wind an earthquake, but* the LORD was not in the earthquake; *and after the earthquake a fire, but* the LORD was not in the fire; *and after the fire* a still small voice *(19:11,12)*.

When Elijah heard the still small voice, he went out and stood at the entrance to the cave, and again God asked him, "What are you doing here, Elijah?" So God was in the still small voice, and spiritually Elijah was back

71

where he had been on Mount Carmel — in holy quietness before God.

Discouragement and fear were gone from Elijah as God sent him to anoint new kings for Syria and Israel and a prophet to succeed him. Then God sent him back to give a message to Ahab, and Elijah went.

Elijah has taken his place in the literature of the world as a great man of God. The New Testament refers to him more than to any other prophet. Whenever he appeared, men had the feeling of God's presence in their midst. Later he appeared out of the "somewhere" to represent the Prophets as Moses represented the Law when Jesus was transfigured on the mount. By that time Elijah *knew* what he never knew on earth — the full wonder of God.

8
THE SPOKESMEN FOR GOD

The idea of the one who loves truth and justice but whose love is greater even than his justice, the idea that man must find his goal by becoming fully human, was carried on by men of vision — the prophets. Their teachings became increasingly impressive because history bore them out. Secular power which reached its peak under Solomon, collapsed after a few centuries, never to be restored in an impressive way. History vindicated those who spoke the truth, not those who held power. [1]

From the day of Elijah to the end of the Old Testament period, the story of God's people is told through their prophets, not through their political leaders. Only a few of the kings were faithful to God. Wealth, prestige, power, and pleasure possessed king and people alike. Religion was made a handmaid to selfish interests. The people who remembered the covenant repeated through the generations forgot the commission that accompanied it. Urbanization increased the contrast between rich and poor. Those in power exploited the downtrodden and helpless. The nation no longer lived as the "people of God." It is a marvel that in that period of spiritual deterioration anyone could see clearly enough to discern the will of God for His chosen people. But in spite of all the religious confusion, there was always a continuity of prophethood in Israel and Judah.

The prophets saw God as the God of all nations and therefore not the private God of the "sons of Abraham," to be used by them for their special privilege. They would not be "saved" simply because of their religious heritage. This was religious heresy to the "orthodox" religious establishment.

But even more flagrant was the prophets' discerning message that God was the God of all life — that He expected religion to have a consistent bearing on all social life, on all business transactions, and on all political life. This was especially pertinent because they were established as a "nation under God." A prophet who dared to expose the sins of the establishment was quickly accused of treason. He carried the burden of being misunderstood as God was misunderstood. The true prophet of God was bound to live a lonely and dangerous life.

The last forty years of the eighth century B.C. produced four great prophets. Amos and Hosea were preaching in the northern kingdom, Isaiah and Micah in the southern kingdom.

Amos

Amos was the most unlikely of prophets. No vocational guidance expert would ever have found him. When Amaziah, the priest of Bethel, told Amos to return home to prophesy, he answered, "I am no prophet, nor a prophet's son; but I am a herdsman, and a dresser of sycamore trees, and the LORD took me from following the flock, and the LORD said to me, 'Go, prophesy to my people Israel.' Now therefore hear the word of the LORD" (Amos 7:14-16).

Amos had so much assurance in the Lord that he had the courage to speak even to a professional in religion, the priest! Not only was Amos a herdsman from a rugged country, but he found himself a southerner attacking the North for their sins. He was a prophet of doom to a people who felt secure in their power and wealth.

The message of Amos was as rugged as the life he had lived in his native Tekoa. In the quiet of the countryside he had a listening ear for his God. He knew the Scriptures, the story of his people and their God. He may have sold his wool in Samaria and Bethel. At least he knew of the unprecedented prosperity of the North; he knew of their luxury and self-indulgence gained through injustice and oppression. He saw the emptiness and farce of their religious worship. He knew that religious prostitution could not be true worship of a holy God. With all he saw, he was sure of one thing — godlessness spells the doom of any people. So he warned them of the doom to come, challenging them to honest faith in Jehovah God. No wonder a self-satisfied, proud priest would send him home. When Amos found the people unwilling to listen, he did go home and wrote down the messages God had given him.

Through the centuries when men have gone to the Bible for encouragement in their struggle for the liberation of the underprivileged, they have found courage in the message which Amos received from God and then wrote down.

Hosea

Hosea was the next man God sent to Israel. The doom foreseen by Amos was already coming to pass. He prophesied in the early years of Jereboam II when prosperity was at its height, but Hosea witnessed the tragedies that befell Israel's fortunes. Hosea was of the North and had a natural concern for his people and his nation. The revolt, anarchy, and bloodshed in his nation broke his heart. The increasing tragedies did not bring the people back to God. Religion became even more corrupt. Highway robbery and organized vice were actually directed by the priests. Fear and uncertainty gripped the people. Family life had gone to pieces. The temple prostitutes were always available to men "worshipers." Men even discovered their own wives taking part in the temple prostitution.

Hosea was as discerning as Amos, but he had also developed an underlying tenderness. He is called the "prophet of love." His message came out of his heart experience of God.

Hosea had come into an understanding of the love of God that had never been perceived by preceding prophets, but he had paid the price for that discernment in his own experience of love. He was naturally a tender-hearted man, and he had fallen in love with a beautiful woman, whom he married. They had three children. His wife, Gomer, had the same problem many women still have, the famous "problem that has no name." She grew restless with her life at home and finally ran away with another man. Time passed, but Hosea never ceased to love her and long for her.

Then one day he was shocked to see Gomer in a wretched condition and up for sale on the slave market. She was a discarded woman by this time, but not by Hosea. In spite of all her sin, he bought her back and reinstated her in his home as his wife and as the mother of their three children. Then tender-hearted Hosea realized that if he could love Gomer after all that had happened, how much more must God love Israel, who had also played the harlot!

Hosea learned how love suffers, and he saw how God suffered when His chosen people failed Him. Hosea found a balance between justice and love which deepened his understanding of God. He discovered that real strength was involved in forgiveness; he could see how God was not minimizing sin when He could forgive a repentant people. No other nation had any idea of such a God of love. To Hosea, sin was unfaithfulness, but genuine repentance would bring forgiveness from the God who loves His people.

Micah

While Amos and Hosea ministered in the northern kingdom, Micah and Isaiah were called to be prophets in the southern kingdom. Micah, like Amos, was a countryman, but his home was in the fertile areas where farming was more profitable. Micah, however, was as one of the poor. He knew how the poor were fleeced by the rich. His nation was ready for collapse. Idolatry, superstition, soothsaying, and witchcraft were everywhere in the land. (Sounds like modern times!)

Micah was sure of his experience of God and of the guidance God had given him:

> But as for me, I am filled with power
> Through the Spirit of the Lord!
> I can see what is just and right,
> And I have the strength to declare it.
> (Mic. 3:8 Phillips).

He spoke clearly to the people about how they hated the right and twisted what was straight, how they filled Zion with bloodshed and Jerusalem with crime, how their leaders dispensed justice at a price, how the priests taught what they were paid to teach, and how the prophets managed to get visions according to the fees they were paid.

But in spite of a seemingly hopeless situation Micah could anticipate a day when people would truly seek their God:

> And he will judge between great peoples,
> And make decision between nations far and wide.

Then they shall hammer their swords into
  ploughshares,
And their spears into pruning-hooks.
Nation shall lift no sword against nation,
And never again will they learn to make war.
Every man shall live beneath the shade of his
  own vine and fig-tree,
And no one shall make him afraid.
The Lord of hosts has declared this with his own
  voice! (4:3,4 Phillips).

We know this hasn't had a chance to happen yet, but it *is* the voice and will of God, and *God is waiting for people to live by the laws of the Creator*.

Isaiah

Isaiah was the greatest of all the prophets. He knew that God is the hero of all scriptural history and that it is God who determines the final outcome of history. Like the other true prophets, he knew that real peace and prosperity cannot be achieved except by living according to the will and plan of God. He recognized man's injustice as being against God more than against man.

Isaiah was a statesman. He belonged to the court circle and was well acquainted with kings and other high officials. He knew their relationships with surrounding nations. He was well educated in his religion and devout in his worship of the Lord, so he was prepared and available when God needed him. One day, about 740 B.C., the year in which King Uzziah died, Isaiah was in the temple to worship when the Lord came to him. Here is the story:

I saw the Lord seated high on a lofty throne, while the train of his robes flowed over the temple floor. Seraphs hovered around him, each with six wings — two to cover their faces, two to cover their feet and two to keep them in the air. They kept calling to each other crying:

Holy, holy, holy is the Lord of hosts
The whole earth is full of his glory.

The doorway shook to its foundations at the sound of their voices, and smoke began to fill the temple (Isa. 6:1-4 Phillips).

The most wonderful experience that can happen to anyone is to come into such a consciousness of the living God. After this experience one can never be the same again; life is indeed lived on another plane. It becomes *natural* to think in terms of the kingdom of God and to be a part of it. But the first reaction is always a feeling of unworthiness, sinfulness, and uncleanness in contrast to the holiness of God. No wonder Isaiah cried out:

Alas for me — for I am finished! I am a foul-mouthed man and I live among a foul-mouthed people. For with my own eyes I have seen the King, the Lord of hosts. Then one of the seraphs flew toward me carrying a red-hot coal which he had taken with tongs from the altar. With this he touched my mouth saying, See, now your guilt shall go and your sin be forgiven! (6:5-7 Phillips).

The cleansing was to make Isaiah whole (meaning

the same as *holy)* and to set him free to go out with God's message. Such an experience is never for the person alone, but is always preparation for service. Again, it was a call, a covenant, and then a commission. Isaiah added, "Then I heard the voice of the Lord, saying: Whom shall I send? Who will go for us?" Of course by now Isaiah was ready to respond, "Here am I: send me" (6:8,9 *Phillips).*

Then Isaiah was told that even though he would go with God's message, the people were not ready to listen. Isaiah was to truly enter into the experience of God — to go to the people with the love of God and to have that message spurned. But Isaiah was ready. God would not have to wait alone.

Isaiah had lived in the midst of politics, and after his wonderful experience of God he did not "withdraw" into the "religious field," but was able with his new discernment to judge the whole political field according to God's kingdom principles. He realized that God is sovereign over the whole world and that He desires His people to represent Him in this world.

Isaiah knew human nature so well — the pull of power, prestige, pleasure — that he saw how hard it had become for people in their sin of self-centeredness to turn to God; no more than a remnant would respond to God in humble faithfulness. The only hope he could see was through some intervention by God's grace. He believed that God would send an Anointed One, a Savior, a Messiah to help his people. A new age could come only by God's grace.

He knew politics, but he told the kings of Judah

81

that if they turned to Egypt or any other nation for help they would only meet defeat, and that the only way to succeed as a nation was to trust in God. In fact this is the point in the famous seventh chapter where God gives the promise of a son, Immanuel (meaning ''God with us''), as His sign to the faithful.

Isaiah believed in this coming day of the Lord:

The people who moved in darkness
Have seen a shining light;
Upon those who lived in the land
*   of the shadow of death*
The light has shown! . . .

For to us a child will be born,
To us a son will be given;
And the government rests upon his shoulders,
And his name shall be:
Wonderful Counsellor,
Mighty God,
Everlasting Father,
Prince of Peace.
His power shall spread unceasingly
And his peace shall not be broken (9:2,6,7
Phillips).

Isaiah saw that before that great day would come, much trouble would befall the people because of their disobedience; they had brought evil upon themselves. Isaiah lived to see Jerusalem spared, but the wickedness of later kings spoiled the work of God. Manasseh's fifty-five-year reign of evil could not be wiped out by the reforms of his grandson Josiah, because there had been no real change in the hearts of the people.

Jeremiah

All these tragedies were witnessed by the next great prophet, Jeremiah, who ministered with a broken heart. He, too, was of the aristocracy, a priest. He was brought up in the quiet company of scholars, priests, and students of the Scriptures. He also had a definite experience of God in his call to be a prophet (Jer. 1:4-10).

Jeremiah, indeed, entered into the heartache of God as he spoke for the Lord:

> *For my people have committed two evils; they have forsaken me, the fountain of living waters, and hewed out cisterns for themselves, broken cisterns, that can hold no water (Jer. 2:13).*

As God's spokesman, Jeremiah was constantly going against the current of his day. He had to cry out, "Why does the way of the wicked prosper? Why do all who are treacherous thrive?" (12:1). At a later time the Lord answered him, "Behold, I am the LORD, the God of all flesh; is anything too hard for me?" (32:27).

Jeremiah saw the best of his people led into captivity in 598 B.C. Even the sacred vessels and all the wealth were taken. Daniel and Ezekiel, also men of God, were with the captives in Babylon while Habakkuk was left with Jeremiah in Jerusalem. With all his suffering, even imprisonment for "treason," Jeremiah saw that the old covenant had become worthless and that God would have to make a new covenant. This new covenant would be an inner law: I will put my law within them, and I will write it upon their hearts; and I will be their

God, and they shall be my people (31:33).

In spite of everything, Jeremiah had hope because he believed in God and His Word.

And God still waited for His people to turn to Him.

Ezekiel

For the people in Babylonian captivity, conditions were deplorable. God came to Ezekiel, another aristocrat, and called him to service. God came to him in visions (Ezek. 1:28; 2:2).

Then Ezekiel was told that he was to give the Lord's message whether the people listened or not. Usually the people did not listen. But in the most discouraging moment God gave Ezekiel the vision of the valley of dry bones (chap. 37). Old, dry bones were scattered through a valley. Ezekiel was told to prophesy to the bones, and he obeyed. There was a rattling sound, the bones came together, flesh came on them, and then breath came into them! Then the Lord said, "Son of man, these bones are the whole house of Israel. . . . O my people, and I will bring you home into the land of Israel. And you shall know that I am the LORD. . . . And I will put my Spirit within you, and you shall live" (37:11-14).

We have the same Lord who appeared to Ezekiel, and it is still true that only through His Spirit can real life come to the church. Seventeen-year-old Laura, in her new-found joy in the Lord, was not prepared to have patience with older folk who clung to old patterns in the church. One Sunday she said to me, "I'm going to another church; these people are hopeless." I said,

84

"This is no time for you to leave; this is when they need you." I asked her to read the story of the valley of dry bones. She read it and came back with a faith twinkle in her eyes.

From a human standpoint the "people of God" were in a hopeless situation. They had lost everything, and they had nothing to return to in the land of their fathers. They were in captivity, without any hope for the future. Only because of his faith in God could Ezekiel have any hope for his people.

Nehemiah and Ezra

In captivity, without their temple, some of the people did find God through a new study of the Scriptures and through their fellowship with one another. God used King Cyrus after he conquered Babylon, even though Cyrus did not know it. Cyrus sent many of the exiles back to their homeland and gave them money to rebuild their temple. After the dedication of this temple in 516 B.C., almost nothing is known of the little community in Jerusalem for over sixty years. Then God brought Nehemiah and Ezra to them. Nehemiah rebuilt the walls of Jerusalem, and Ezra taught the people God's Word in the Scriptures. But conditions did not improve much, and the people continued to be rebellious.

Malachi

Malachi, the last of the prophets, appeared like the last ray of a setting sun. He cried out against the futility of superficial worship which masqueraded as the real thing. The people did not see that they were robbing God. Malachi answered, "Bring the full tithes into the storehouse, that there may be food in my house; and thereby put me to the test, says the LORD of hosts, if I will not open the windows of heaven for you and pour down for you an overflowing blessing" (Mal. 3:10). Then the Lord promised that He would send another "Elijah" to change the hearts of the fathers and the children.

This is the last direct word we have recorded from God through a prophet until the time of John the Baptist. All that the people of Israel had to go on was the promise of a Deliverer who would come to bless them.
Again God waited.

[1]Fromm, *You Shall Be As Gods*, p. 91.

9
ERA OF FAITH ADJUSTMENT

During the centuries between the Old and New Testaments, faithful Jews may have felt that God was hiding, because no prophet came saying, "Thus saith the Lord"; but God was as present as ever, whether the people knew it or not. He was waiting for them to learn new lessons of faith. Political upheavals and defeats devastated any faith in security through a political nation.

Between the seventh and second centuries B.C. the world saw the rise and then the collapse and disappearance of six great world empires: Assyria, Babylon, Persia, Macedonia, the Seleucid and Ptolemaic kingdoms. With them died their religions and their culture, leaving behind an indelible imprint on the civilizations that were to come. Throughout all the changes of this time of upheaval, the Jews survived, a distinct cultural and religious entity, indestructible in the face of all vicissitudes.[1]

During the time of captivity away from the temple, their center of worship, the Jews began to gather together as groups to discuss their situation and to encourage one another. These group meetings developed into the synagogue movement. Even after the return of many to Jerusalem and the rebuilding of the temple, they continued the synagogue custom. The synagogue became a place for study of the Scriptures even more than a place of worship. The study of the Scriptures, both the Law and the Prophets, was now available *to all the people*, instead of only to the leaders.

In captivity the people somehow realized that their identity as a nation depended upon their faithfulness to one God. A new sense of individual responsibility developed when they no longer felt that they were merely a small part of a national response. Those who returned from captivity did not return just because the crowd returned. They needed a new kind of individual commitment, for even in a foreign land they were not kept in slavery, and many were prosperous and comfortable. Those who returned to the "homeland," which many of them had never seen, had a willingness to sacrifice opportunities for making a living in order to serve their God. It also meant a long, difficult journey, walking nine hundred miles over a six-month period. So they became a religious community rather than a political body.

Ezra and Nehemiah were the two men who felt led

of God to serve the people who returned.

> *Ezra built the wall of the Law around the people and Nehemiah erected a wall of stone to protect the city. One was designed to shut out pagan ideas and the other was raised as a defense against invaders. Both were defensive in purpose but each was somewhat static by nature. Neither fulfilled completely the purpose for which it was intended. Truth tended to become crystallized and was reduced to definitions and boiled down to dogmas among the Jews. Righteousness was thought out in terms of rules and right doctrine. Ezra and Nehemiah elevated their homeland to a good defensive position and set the course for its future. Jews became thereafter largely a people of the Law, of rules and regulations. Perhaps this was necessary for an interim period but in the long view it almost smothered the vital spirit of creative faith.*[2]

There also followed encroachments on the religious life of the Jews. Under Antiochus IV the high priesthood of the temple was sold to the highest bidder, and the high priest became a tool of whatever king was in control. There was a period of the dangerous game of politics. Some of the people wanted to be "up-to-date" and cooperate with the ruling powers, but many more rebelled. This rebellion led to the successful Maccabean revolt, which gave the Jews a period of political independence during the time of the Hasmonian dynasty (143-63 B.C.), but this was only a time of transition. There was still no accepted orthodoxy within Judaism, but their growing desire to be obedient to their Law kept them rather steady through this period of religious and social crisis. This crisis situation developed out of the conflict that resulted from external social and political influence as it related to their exclusive religious faith.

The emphasis on God did endure, and they became "strong in the faith" largely through the stimulation of the Pharisees, who became a strong party during this period. The Pharisaic emphasis on the Law and the Prophets helped to make the rank and file of the people into a "people of the Book." Even though the classic voice of inspired prophecy was silent, from the time of Ezra existing Scripture became the subject of intensive study. But in a changing culture the Law needed to be reinterpreted, and this became the task of the Pharisees and the scribes. Religion was not static and the Law was not fixed, so these men became rather free in their minute interpretations. Even though they still believed in God's control over history, it was easy to make the observance of the Law an end in itself rather than remembering the scriptural emphasis on the prior relationship to God. Then, as now, the emphasis on the Book as an end in itself led to a severe legalism.

It is only because of those who fell into this subtle trap, even though they may have been sincere, that Christians have come to think of Pharisaism as synonymous with hypocrisy. This really is not fair to the Pharisees. Jesus did not criticize them because they were Pharisees. He criticized the ones who had *vested religious interests* and so were not to be trusted as spiritual guides.

Some years ago the Jewish rabbis of the West Side in Chicago invited all Christian pastors and theological seminary professors to a weekend institute. One of their main concerns was to explain that Judaism lives today because of the spiritual leadership of Pharisees. We owe this respect to the people of "the Book" even though they are not ready to take the New Testament as a fulfillment of "the Book." In Christianity also too many people think of the Bible as an end in itself and seem to know nothing of the basic relationship to a heavenly Father.

As the elevation of the Law took precedence over prophetic utterance in religious experience, God's Word *as written* became more and more important. They did not see earthly hope for the fulfillment of God's promises to His chosen people, so there was a growing belief that only through divine intervention could these promises be fulfilled. A strong theological hope that a Messiah would come to bring in the promised kingdom gave the people a security they might not have had otherwise. To them this meant a time when God's rule would be accepted. It was much more than a geographical statement to the faithful.

Before the Exile, nationalism had become the main concern, but after the Exile, with the emphasis on Scripture interpretation, different parties arose. The Pharisees were the Scripture interpreters, while the Sadducees protected the ritual worship. The Sadducees, who were from the upper classes, denied the Resurrection as well as the existence of angels and demons. Although the Pharisees believed in nonviolence, they had no love for Greece and Rome; but the Sadducees accommodated themselves to Rome and could often intercede for their people. With the destruction of the temple in A.D. 70 the influence of the Sadducees was wiped out and the future of Judaism rested with the Pharisees.

The Essenes were another group of devout Jews. They withdrew from all society to find God in the wilderness. They had no interest in the temple rituals but gave themselves to the study of Scripture and to disciplined devotion and daily living. Since the discovery of the Dead Sea Scrolls, we know much of their life and thought. From them we now have a complete copy of Isaiah dating from 100 B.C. (nine hundred years older than any previous copy). The end of the Essene community came also in A.D. 70.

The Zealots were not only zealous for the Law of God, but they were ready to die for their faith, even to full revolt against their heathen oppressors. They were revolutionary religious extremists. The description of their spirit sounds much like some of the violent ones today who are "theologically orthodox" but spiritually unorthodox.

All groups looked for a Messiah, even though their expectations varied.

Another change in Jewish culture was in the matter of language. In the Grecian era many Jews spoke Greek as well as Aramaic, which they had used since the earliest days. Because so many Jews spoke Greek, scholars in Alexandria translated the Hebrew Scriptures into Greek. This translation is known as the Septuagint and is the version most quoted by New Testament writers. The use of Greek gave the Jews an almost universal language. As their religious devotion increased, they developed a missionary zeal which took them everywhere among Greek-speaking peoples. In fact, many of them became more fanatical than pious.

In 63 B.C., when Rome conquered Jerusalem, permission was granted for individual religious freedom. Even though Rome had conquered Greece, Rome was conquered by Grecian culture and so became the chief transmitter of Hellenistic culture. Wherever the Roman Empire was extended, Roman roads followed. So Rome provided the media for a whole new era of newscasting.

By the end of the first century B.C., spiritual hunger, expectancy of a Deliverer, new communication possibilities, and a remnant of the faithful converged into what the apostle Paul called the "fullness of time" (Gal. 4:4). And the voice of God reached through to man again. The long silence was over (or what *seemed* to be silence).

Before I made a study of the "intertestamental period," I thought of it as a barren period — just an "in-between time." But the fact is that it was a creative era when God was truly at work *waiting* for His people to learn more than childlike obedience. They were learning to think, to stand in the midst of conflicting cultures, to know their Scriptures. It is true they had not learned that *faith does not develop from argument,* and many of them followed the law so legalistically that their faith had little to do with God. The law had lost

93

touch with religious experience, but the fanatical contenders for the law did not know what they were missing.

Still there remained a remnant of faithful ones, mostly the simple folk. They had an abiding faith in God, the God of their fathers. They also were waiting for something to happen. And they were the very ones through whom it happened.

Considering the life of Jesus and the fact that He was a layman with "no right" to enter the inner courts of the temple, it is interesting that the first announcement of His coming was made to a priest, Zechariah, while he was on duty in the temple. But Zechariah and his wife were both righteous before God, walking in all the commandments and ordinances of the Lord, blameless, and with hearts ready to receive the long-awaited announcement.

The seeming silence of centuries was broken.

An angel appeared to the right of the altar of incense. Zechariah was frightened. A true messenger from God always *allays* fear, so the first words were "Do not be afraid." Then Zechariah was told he and his wife were to have a son who would prepare the way for the Lord and that his name should be John. This was too good to be true, Zechariah thought; his wife, Elizabeth, was barren, and they were both too old to have a child. He exclaimed, "How shall I know this?" The angel answered,

> *I am Gabriel, who stand in the presence of God; and I was sent to speak to you, and to bring you this good news. And behold, you will be silent and*

unable to speak until the day that these things come to pass, because you did not believe my words, which will be fulfilled in their time (Luke 1:19,20).

Many people were waiting in worship for Zechariah to come out of the temple, and they wondered at his delay. When he did come, they perceived that he had seen a vision. Zechariah finished his time of ministry in the temple and then returned to his wife. For nine months he was unable to speak, and I am sure this must have been a time of reverential awe before the wonder of the power of God. When the baby boy was born and the time came for him to be named, Elizabeth said his name was John. The neighbors could not believe this. Surely Zechariah would have him named for himself according to their custom. But Zechariah wrote on a tablet, "His name is John." Zechariah's quiet faith in God answered the neighbors as his speech was restored.

The second heavenly announcement was to a teen-ager. She, too, was frightened. The angel Gabriel said to her, "Do not be afraid, Mary, for you have found favor with God" (Luke 1:30). Then the angel told this girl she was to have a child and His name was to be Jesus. His name would be great, and He would be called the Son of the Most High. The angel added this beautiful explanation: "The Holy Spirit will come upon you, and the power of the Most High will overshadow you; therefore the child to be born will be called holy, the Son of God. . . . For with God nothing will be impossible" (vv. 35,37). Considering what Mary, not yet married, might have to face from people, her answer to the angel is one of the world's greatest statements of devotion to God: "Behold, I am the handmaid of the Lord; let it be to me according to your word" (v. 38).

The angel Gabriel had even made an announcement for Elizabeth: "And behold, your kinswoman Elizabeth in her old age has also conceived a son; and this is the sixth month with her who was called barren" (v. 36). Mary needed to talk to someone who would understand, so she went to visit Elizabeth who lived one hundred miles away. When Mary arrived, Elizabeth was inspired to praise God and to recognize Mary's condition. Mary was also inspired to praise God:

My soul magnifies the Lord, and my spirit rejoices in God my Savior, for he has regarded the low estate of his handmaiden. For behold, henceforth all generations will call me blessed; for he who is mighty has done great things for me, and holy is his name (vv. 46-49).

Mary stayed with Elizabeth for three months. There was no generation gap between them, even though they differed so much in age, not only because they were both "expecting," but because each had an experience of God.

There was another heavenly announcement, an announcement of explanation, that had to be made. Mary's betrothed husband, Joseph, was a just man. Under the circumstances and because of his moral integrity, he had to divorce her. He was kind and did not want to shame her, so he was going to do it quietly. He had this on his mind as he went to sleep. In a dream the angel came to him, saying, "Joseph, son of David, do not fear to take Mary as your wife, for that which is conceived in her is of the Holy Spirit; she will bear a son, and you shall call his name Jesus, for he will save his people from their sins" (Matt. 1:20,21). So Joseph also entered into the purpose of God for the coming of the promised and long-awaited Savior. All we know about Joseph is that he never spoiled the word *father* — he kept it clean so that Jesus could use the word for the heavenly *Father*.

After the birth of Jesus in Bethlehem, the angels again were sent to make an announcement. It was not to kings or priests or those in authority; it was to shepherds out on the hillside. One has to wonder about those shepherds. Did they say Psalm 23 to themselves? Did they read Isaiah and wonder about the coming Savior? Anyway, God knew they had a listening ear (Luke 2:9-14).

The shepherds in their simplicity went to Bethlehem, found the baby Jesus, and worshiped God.

And Mary treasured all these things in her heart, for she was being given sanction after sanction that *her experience of God was authentic* and that she was in God's will.

Simeon and Anna were two old people who spent much time in the temple worshiping God. It had been revealed to Simeon that he would not die until he had seen the promised Messiah, and then it was revealed by the Spirit that the baby brought by Joseph and Mary for the purification ceremony was the Promised One. The parents were amazed as Simeon took the baby in his arms and blessed God (Luke 2:29-32).

The prophetess Anna also came to praise God for this baby.

The strangest visitors of all were the wise men from the Far East. They studied the stars and followed one star in their search for the child born to be "king of the Jews." They found Him and worshiped Him. Since they did not know all the local political complications, they were warned in a dream not to report their findings to Herod, so they went home without seeing him.

These wonderful stories have inspired Christians for centuries. Every Christmas we light a torch of love and good will as people everywhere ponder over them, and many wonder why we don't love all the time if it is possible for a week or more at Christmas.

The record of God's invasion of history has not been written for the sake of argument, for faith does not come from argument. Faith comes — and grows — *as we respond* to God, whether we understand everything or not.

The door is now open for the full revelation of God to be lived before it is written.

[1]Gaalyah Cornfeld, *Daniel to Paul* (New York: Macmillan), pp. 1, 2.

[2]Carl G. Howie, *The Creative Era* (Atlanta: John Knox), p. 16.

10
JESUS, PERFECT REVELATION OF GOD

A December 31, 1971, Associated Press news report said that in 1971 Jesus became the most popular hero on the American scene. Accepting Jesus as a hero is a good idea, because we tend to become like our heroes. But Jesus as a hero is only a starting point; He is so much more than that. He is Savior, and He is the revelation of what it means to be made in the image of God. He is also our example of perfect relationship and perfect experience with God. The present effort to bring Him near to us by emphasizing His humanity is laudable, but it raises a question concerning the definition of humanness.

Some years ago I happened to be standing with three ministers as they were discussing their temptations and shortcomings. One of them said, "But, after all, we are only human." I had an uneasy feeling about that statement. Later I realized that the problem with the statement was its rationalization. We dare not *excuse* our failings because of our humanness. We must *confess* our failings, expecting to grow out of them by God's grace.

In Nazareth of Galilee the idea of Jesus' humanity hit me hard. I realized then that His humanity was much more of a miracle than His divinity. But what did His humanity include? Recently many have included human *weaknesses* in His humanity. It is one thing for people just learning about Jesus to do that, but it is quite another matter when a theologian does it. I am less human when I *yield* to human temptation and frailty; I am more human when the Spirit of God within me helps me conquer irritation, discouragement, and anger. To be fully human Jesus did not have to yield as others do to human weaknesses. It will never do to make Jesus an ordinary human, because *He was not ordinary*. He is truly our Savior, able to help us grow to full maturity in Him, which is true human maturity.

When I was assigned to teach a class on the Life and Teachings of Jesus, I discovered that there was no difference between His life and His teachings. He *was* what He taught. The first and most important fact of His human life was His unquestioned commitment to God. He had deleted all possible questioning as to whether or not He would do God's will. That decision was settled in His life. I can understand that, because when I got married fifty years ago, it was settled in my mind that I would never question my commitment to my husband. When we had differences, I never had to bother about whether I would stay with him or not — the only question was, How do we make it together? Jesus never, therefore, entertained the temptation to be reluctant to do the Father's will. As a human being He always had only one question, "What is my Father's will?"

This commitment to God was a growing experience in Jesus' life. We know little about His youth and maturing manhood, but we do have the story of His time at the temple when He was twelve. He felt at home with the religious teachers there and loved talking with them about God. He even forgot His customary thoughtfulness and obedience to His parents and never noticed when they left for home. When they returned after three days of searching for Him, they could not understand His answer to their anxiety, "How is it that you sought me? Did you not know that I must be in my Father's house?" (Luke 2:49).

In His deepening religious consciousness Jesus did not rebel against His parents but was obedient to them. And "he increased in wisdom and stature, and in favor with God and man" (2:52).

It was eighteen years more before Jesus felt the call to leave His home and the carpenter shop, but these were not wasted years. He was alert to the happenings and hopes of His day. His education in the synagogue was in the Scriptures; He knew the story of His people — their struggles, their failures, their hopes. From His quotations later on, we know that He especially appreciated Deuteronomy and the Prophets. He found His greatest guidance for thought and purpose in Isaiah. He knew that through all the agonies of Israel's history they were still God's chosen people and that through divine intervention God would fulfill all His promises. He knew all the theologies that had developed since the time of the prophets and all the interpretations concerning the promised Messiah. He was a craftsman, and so He knew how to be one with the common people. He loved nature and the things of the land and sea. His later parables were remembered because they were about everyday life. He also knew that God called no man for personal salvation alone, but that everyone was called to be a messenger and a blessing to all people. Those eighteen years were years of waiting for the Father.

Call to Ministry

Then word came about the repentance-baptism ministry of John down south by the Jordan. The people poured in from everywhere — common people, tax collectors, soldiers, and theologians. In no uncertain terms John told them they had failed their God. Some preachers today justify their blatant accusations against their congregations by referring to John's approach, but John's audience was not a captive audience. It was a restless era, and they went out to hear a man from God speak the truth to them. They wanted their faith and hope sustained and validated. So the multitude asked John, ''What shall we do?'' He told them how to change their lives. They asked if he was the Christ, since all people were expecting the Christ. John answered that he was not even worthy to tie the shoes of the One who was coming, One who was much mightier

102

than he. He was only a voice in the wilderness, making the paths straight for the coming of the Lord.

> *Then Jesus came from Galilee to the Jordan to John to be baptized by him. John would have prevented him, saying, "I need to be baptized by you, and do you come to me?" But Jesus answered him, "Let it be so now; for thus it is fitting for us to fulfil all righteousness" (Matt. 3:13-15).*

So Jesus was baptized.

When the two men came up out of the water, Jesus was in prayer, and "the heaven was opened, and the Holy Spirit descended upon him in bodily form, as a dove, and a voice came from heaven, 'Thou art my beloved Son; with thee I am well pleased'" (Luke 3:21,22).

Jesus could have argued against His need of baptism, but He was always guided by a deeper motivation. I once had a teacher who often said, "The greatest evidence of the divinity of Jesus was His unerring instinct to do the right." The voice from heaven assured Him He was doing the right thing. After all, the main experience in baptism is the commitment of one's life to God. In His baptism, Jesus not only identified Himself with the Father but also with all mankind. He was both Son of God and Son of man.

All the convictions that had been developing in the quiet of His private life came to fruition as Jesus yielded to the baptism of John and received the full sanction of the heavenly Father. In the fullness of the Holy Spirit He was led by the Spirit into the wilderness to test out in final form the principles He was to work by in the ministry to which the Father had called Him. There was no *question* in His mind about doing the Father's will, only to discover that will. While at work in Nazareth, He must have thought much about the theological interpretations He had heard all His life about the coming Messiah. In the wilderness He was up against a fixed orthodoxy. Were His growing discernments right? The struggle for clarity through the fog of human limitation was so intense that for over a month He was not even conscious of hunger. When God's will was clear to Him, His answers were automatic; it was *already settled* that He would do God's will. He had no struggle on that point.

As the tension of the struggle ceased, His hunger returned, so, of course, the first temptation was about food. He was in the wilderness without food and far from any market. With His new consciousness of Spirit-power, why shouldn't He turn those round stones into bread? Didn't God provide manna in the wilderness for the children of Israel? The tempter's question was based on the premise: "If you are the Son of God!" Yes, why shouldn't He make bread for Himself? But Jesus *knew* He could never use His special power for Himself. That would break His identification with us. His answer was ready: "Man shall not live by bread alone, but by every word that proceeds from the mouth of God" (Matt. 4:4; cf. Deut. 8:3). Jesus knew that this was not only true for Himself but also for all the people He came to win for the kingdom of God. If He sought to win people by meeting only their physical needs at the outset, they might never know real spiritual hunger.

Later experience proved His discernment to be correct. After He fed the five thousand (John 6:1-15), the people were thrilled at the prospect of having a leader who could provide for all their physical needs, so they attempted to make Him their king. He knew better — He knew the quality of such a following. He did not cash in on this publicity, but withdrew into the quiet of the hills. When the people found Him, He said to them, "You seek me . . . because you ate your fill of the loaves" (6:26). Then He challenged them to seek the spiritual food which endures to eternal life. They asked how to do the will of God. Jesus told them about Moses and the manna and said His Father gives the true bread. When they asked for this bread, He answered, "I am the bread of life; he who comes to me shall not hunger . . ." (6:35). Of course the people retorted, "Is not this Jesus, the son of Joseph, whose father and mother we know?" So easily do the masses turn when they do not get what they think they want!

Another issue in the temptation which became clear at the end of the struggle for guidance and discernment was how to face the expectation of the people for a conquering Messiah. Many men had come proclaiming themselves the promised Messiah but had failed to free the people from foreign kings or the occupying army. From 67 B.C. to 37 B.C. 100,000 men had perished in abortive rebellions. The theologians expected the Messiah to restore the throne of David and the past glories of Israel, while the common people wanted relief from oppression. The temptation was to display power and dazzle men with sensations. If only He would have the faith of the psalmist and dare to go to the pinnacle of the temple and throw himself down. "If you are the son of God, . . . [God] will give his angels charge of you" (Matt. 4:6; cf. Ps. 91:11,12). Other "Messiahs" had lost their followings, but one who showed such evidence of God's care would truly win a following. But Jesus answered, "You shall not tempt the Lord your God."

How clear this discernment was! It was proved true the first time He came back to His hometown. Word had reached the home folk about His miracles and good works in Capernaum and other places. They expected a display of this new power for themselves. He went to the synagogue on the Sabbath day according to His custom; He was not a defiant rebel against the "institution." They honored Him by asking Him to read the Scripture and speak. He read (Luke 4:18-21).

He did not put on a show for them, so they became angry with Him. They tried to put Him out of the city, His hometown, by force, but He just calmly walked away from them. Again they asked, "Is not this Joseph's son?"

The third issue that was clarified for Jesus during His temptation in the wilderness was the method He would use to win a following. The devil showed Him the kingdoms of the world and offered them to Jesus (as if the devil owned them!), if only Jesus would worship him. We hear the same temptation in our day: "Be practical. You know how the people are! Nothing but power works in this world. Get the people in any way you can — and then teach them.'' (One minister said that if the Holy Spirit were taken out of the world, 90 percent of our church work would continue.) Jesus did not accept the nationalistic, power-wielding Messiah concept at all. His concept was illustrated by leaven, salt, light, life, and love. Isaiah's concept of the suffering servant grew on Jesus as He faced the problems of His ministry. The common people and the ''sinners'' were the ones who heard Him gladly. The theologians with their preconceived ideas were the ones who gave Him trouble.

The relationship of Jesus to the heavenly Father was the most outstanding thing in all His religious experience. We look to Jesus not only as Savior, but as the perfect example of the authentic in religious experience of God. If we are going to imitate anyone, we must imitate Him.

The basis of the religious experience of Jesus is expressed in these words: ''I and the Father are one'' (John 10:30), and ''I can do nothing on my own authority; as I hear, I judge; and my judgment is just, because I seek not my own will but the will of him who sent me'' (John 5:30). The fatherhood of God was mentioned by the prophets, but it was more a fatherhood of a nation. Jesus took that name for God and made it His own — and ours.

Jesus never lost sight of the majesty, justice, holiness, and vastness of God; but at the same time He revealed how near God can be in infinite gentleness and love. His prayer life was not a religious discipline; it was a dialogue in love, understanding, and real com-

107

munion. No wonder His disciples asked Him to teach them to pray. They were praying men, but the prayer life of their Master was completely different from the praying they had known.

Jesus taught them what we call the Lord's Prayer. We hear added so often, "But it really was given as the *disciple's* prayer." Actually, in one way it is truly the Lord's prayer, because it is the witness of His experience of the Father: God, the tender Father, approachable, inviting, loving, and still the great Creator of all. It is the witness of His integrity of soul in reverence and worship — "Hallowed be thy name." It is the witness of His own purpose in life followed without compromise or hesitation — "Thy will be done on earth as it is in heaven." He had settled the relationship of the spiritual to the material without any withdrawal from the things of this earth. His incarnation was not only a theological idea; it was a practical daily experience because He was revealing God's interest and love to man. He was the embodiment of loving forgiveness even to the cross, and we cannot be in Christ without that same forgiving spirit. Of course, it is contrary to human nature to love one's enemy — or even to love some neighbors — but Jesus always talked about the possibility of a new nature. Even to theologian Nicodemus, one of the heads of the "church" of his day, Jesus said, "You must be born again." It is impossible to make one's self love some people, but in Christ the new nature makes this love natural. We'll find more of that later.

One of the most creative experiences in the spiritual life of Jesus was His attitude toward sinners. This had never been the experience of devoutly religious people. Perhaps Hosea came nearer to this understanding than anyone else. If he could love Gomer after all her unfaithfulness, surely God would be greater in such love!

What Jesus taught in the Sermon on the Mount was a real witness to His own experience of God as it worked out in His human relationships. We have seen His purity of heart or singleness of purpose and His passionate desire to do the Father's will; we know He was a peacemaker and that He was persecuted for righteousness' sake; but few people seem to know what he meant by "poor in spirit" and by meekness. People ridicule the meek. They think it means to stand passively before whatever happens to them without dignity or positive spirit. The fact is that one cannot be meek as Jesus was without an unquestioned security in God and the assured dignity which sets one free to forget self. Then one is above the fear of competition or any need for *self*-defense.

That brings to mind the picture of Jesus standing before Pilate; Pilate had the power to condemn Him, but Jesus made no defense. (After nineteen hundred years, history says Pilate was standing in judgment before Jesus.) Jesus stood there with complete poise. He was more sensitive than any other man; He felt more deeply than any man can feel; He knew the human danger that faced Him with a full understanding of the bewilderment of those who loved Him. Still, He was poised. Such poise is the perfect balance of all emotions, possible only in the power and strength of the Holy Spirit.

The greatest misrepresentation of Jesus is in men's interpretation of the cleansing of the temple. Even preachers justify their own "righteous" anger by picturing Jesus as "losing His temper" in the temple that day. A loss of temper even in a righteous cause was not consistent with His divinely natural poise. He was capable of deeper emotion than any other man, and He could show it and still maintain His poise.

Every time Jesus went to the temple, from His boyhood days on, He must have felt deeply about those buyers and sellers in the house of prayer. The excuse was to have the animals near for worshipers who wanted to buy for their sacrifice. And Jews from afar had to have their money changed into temple coins. There was the noise of bleating animals and the cooing of doves plus frequent cheating among the moneychangers. But even more distressing than these transactions was the fact that this business was going on in the court of the Gentiles. This meant that there was no longer room for Gentiles seeking to worship in the temple. Mark tells us that Jesus said, "My house shall be called a house of prayer for all the nations" (Mark 11:17). This was hard for Jesus to endure in a house called God's house.

What Jesus did was not the result of a sudden outburst. The hour of crisis had come for Him. The day before as He had entered the city, He had entered with a breaking heart. "And when he drew near and saw the city he wept over it, saying, 'Would that even today

110

you knew the things that make for peace! . . . you did not know the time of your visitation'" (Luke 19:41,44). "And he entered Jerusalem, and went into the temple; and when he had looked round at everything, as it was already late, he went out to Bethany with the twelve" (Mark 11:11). The next day they returned to Jerusalem, and again Jesus entered the temple, "and [he] began to drive out those who sold and those who bought in the temple, and he overturned the tables of the money-changers and the seats of those who sold pigeons; and he would not allow any one to carry anything through the temple" (Mark 11:15,16).

If this had been merely an act of force, the people of the temple could easily have stopped Him. Why did they let Him get away with it? They knew they were in the wrong, and now the true spirit of God's house challenged them. So they left. Throughout His ministry the people recognized an authority in Jesus, not an overpowering authority but the authority of truth that makes argument, force, or defense irrelevant.

Jesus was popular with the common people, and because of this popularity, He knew that the religious authorities were growing stronger and stronger in their opposition to Him. They watched Him and set traps to catch Him. One wonders at His poise and assurance under the gaze of critical watching eyes at the edge of every crowd, but He was unaffected by their growing antagonism, so sure was He of His heavenly Father's will. He spent many nights in prayer that His disciples never recorded.

One time after prayer He asked His disciples what

111

people said about Him, and then of them He asked, "But who do you say that I am?" (Matt. 16:13-28; Mark 8:27–9:1; Luke 9:18-27). This is the time that Peter said, "You are the Christ, the Son of the living God." Then Jesus began to tell them what He knew was going to happen: suffering, rejection, and the cross. This did not fit into the disciples' understanding of the Messiah, so Peter dared to rebuke his Master. Jesus said to Peter, "You are not looking at things from God's point of view, but from man's" (Mark 8:32 Phillips). Then Jesus said to the multitude with His disciples: "If any man would come after me, let him deny himself and take up his cross and follow me. For whoever would save his life will lose it; and whoever loses his life for my sake and the gospel's will save it" (Mark 8:34,35). Many people think this law of life which Jesus lived is the opposite of life and personal fulfillment. Only those who know that this is the *only way to fulfillment* can understand the depth and quality of Jesus' spiritual experience. God's way of thinking is often the opposite of man's. The cross is more than jewelry or decoration in a church; it is a way of life.

After this acceptance of the cross in His life, Jesus again had great assurance from the Father that He was on the right path. So, a week later Jesus took Peter, James, and John with Him up on the mountain to pray. And as Jesus was praying, "the appearance of his countenance was altered, and his raiment became dazzling white. And behold, two men talked with him, Moses and Elijah, who appeared in glory and spoke of his departure, which he was to accomplish at Jerusalem'' (Luke 9:29-31). Of course, Peter had to speak up, and while he was still speaking a cloud overshadowed them, and a voice from out of the cloud said, ''This is my beloved Son, with whom I am well pleased; listen to him'' (Matt. 17:5). The three disciples fell on their faces and were filled with awe. But Jesus came and touched them, saying, ''Rise, and have no fear'' (v. 7; 2 Peter 1:13-18). They came down from the mountain to earthly tragedies and weaknesses again, but Jesus was once more assured of the Father's pleasure in Him. With such assurance He could face anything.

Jesus and His disciples went on to Galilee where He sought privacy with them in order to teach them. Again He said to them, ''Let these words sink into your ears; for the Son of man is to be delivered into the hands of men'' (Luke 9:44). Still the disciples could not understand that this meant tragedy. Surely their Master had the power to escape danger. Surely He was planning for victory as they dreamed of it. So as they traveled along the road, they fell to discussing among themselves which one of them would be the greatest in the coming kingdom. Jesus perceived their thoughts, so He sat down, called them to Him, and said, ''If any one would be first, he must be last of all and servant of all'' (Mark 9:35). This still seemed foolish to the disciples. And to this day, that is the last concept followers of Jesus are able to understand, because it's God's way of thinking and not man's.

The Last Week

"When the days drew near for him to be received up, he set his face to go to Jerusalem" (Luke 9:51). As Jesus and His men went through Samaria on the way to Jerusalem, the Samaritans would not let them stop over because Jesus set His face toward Jerusalem. James and John couldn't take this rebuff; they wanted to call down fire on the people and have them destroyed; but Jesus rebuked the two disciples, and they went on to another village. The slowness of the disciples to understand Him must have been harder on Jesus than the enmity of the jealous authorities. But through it all He was unwavering in His relationship with God. At the tomb of Lazarus, *before* the answer to His prayer He said, "Father, I thank thee that thou hast heard me. I knew that thou hearest me always . . ." (John 11:41,42).

As they neared Jerusalem, Jesus told His disciples again about coming events: "The Son of man will be delivered to the chief priests and scribes, and they will condemn him to death, and deliver him to the Gentiles to be mocked and scourged and crucified, and he will be raised on the third day" (Matt. 20:18,19). They could not fathom the possibility of His death, so they did not take note of the promised Resurrection. Again the striving for first place showed itself. James and John, for themselves or through their mother, asked for first place on each side of Jesus as He came into the kingdom. This would push Peter out! Jesus told them they did not know what they were asking. They were still thinking of a temporal kingdom.

On Sunday as they entered Jerusalem, Jesus let the

people have their way in His "triumphal entry"; but the greatest triumph was not the glory given to Jesus. The triumph was that He could let the people *do this* knowing what tragedies the week would bring. He saw their blindness and wept over the city that did not know the day of its visitation.

Then followed strenuous days. He dared with dignity to cleanse the temple. The chief priests, scribes, and elders challenged the authority of His teaching and His acts. He dared to advise the people and His disciples to practice what the scribes and Pharisees *taught* but not what they *did,* for they did not practice what they preached. Often their holiness was mere pretense.

Through all the leaders of the "faith" did to Him, Jesus' agony was never for Himself — only for them in their blindness: "O Jerusalem, Jerusalem, killing the prophets and stoning those who are sent to you! How often would I have gathered your children together as a hen gathers her brood under her wings, and you would not!" (Matt. 23:37).

One bright spot of this last week was the coming of the Greeks to see Him, but Jesus could only say to them that the end was near: "The hour has come for the Son of man to be glorified. Truly, truly, I say to you, unless a grain of wheat falls into the earth and dies, it remains alone; but if it dies, it bears much fruit . . ." (John 12:23,24). Then the awfulness of the Cross hit Him anew. He said, "Now is my soul troubled. And what shall I say? 'Father, save me from this hour'? No, for this purpose I have come to this hour. Father, glorify thy name" (12:27,28). The voice of assurance came

115

again, but Jesus really did not need it. He said it came for the people and not for Him. Then He added, "And I, when I am lifted up from the earth, will draw all men unto myself" (v. 32). How hard it is for us to learn the difference between drawing people and forcing them.

Jesus did much teaching during that last week, but perhaps the most important time was on Passover night when He was alone with His disciples. These were His last hours with them as a group before His death, and His first act was consistent with His whole life: He took a towel, as a servant would, and washed their feet. He ate with them and had communion with them, which they did not understand. I think the meaning of communion hit me hardest during the communion at the opening worship service of the meeting of our national church board. The minister asked each one of us to say as we passed the bread to the next person, "This bread is the communion of the body of Christ *which I have broken.*" And for the cup, "This cup is the communion of the blood of Christ *which I have spilled.*" After prayer he laid the bread and the cup on the table and said, "This table from which we have taken the bread and the cup is the table on which we will do the work of the church this week." That board meeting was of a different quality from any I ever attended.

Jesus knew what His suffering and death would mean to His disciples, and He had to prepare them as much as possible. He could go in seeming defeat and leave them in despair because He had faith in the coming of the Holy Spirit. He told them He would not leave them desolate, that He would come to them. He told them, "It is to your advantage that I go away, for if I do not go away, the Counselor will not come to you; but if I go, I will send him to you" (John 16:7). The Counselor was not to come as a substitute for Jesus but as the agent of His Presence. He told them, "Peace I leave with you; my peace I give to you; not as the world gives do I give to you. Let not your hearts be troubled, neither let them be afraid" (14:27). His peace was not a peace in the absence of conflict but in the midst of it. He said this when He knew He was going to be murdered the next day!

Then they went out into the Garden of Gethsemane, and Jesus took Peter, James, and John over to a quiet area to pray. He asked them to watch with Him, saying, "My soul is very sorrowful, even to death; remain here, and watch with me" (Matt. 26:38). They were so blind to the situation that they did not recognize His distress, even though Peter had pledged his love even to death. Jesus fell on the ground and prayed that if it were possible the hour might pass from Him. Just before the beginning of His ministry Jesus faced all the significance of the work before Him. Now He was at the end of that ministry, facing the worst human suffering and shame. Was it really the Father's will? He prayed, "Father, if thou art willing, remove this cup from me; nevertheless not my will, but thine, be done" (Luke 22:42). An angel from heaven came and strengthened Him. And being in agony He prayed more earnestly, and His sweat came like great drops of blood falling upon the ground. Then He rose and found the three sleeping. The second and the third times He prayed the same prayer, and still they slept. At last He told them to get up, that His betrayer was at hand. This woke them, still not knowing what He meant.

But after that time of prayer, Jesus was indeed ready to meet the worst: betrayal by one disciple, denial by another, flight of others, false accusations in an unjust trial, scourging and other untold suffering, the gloating over Him of the jealous religious leaders of His people, the misunderstanding and despair of the common people who loved Him, and finally the most disgraceful death of His day — to be hanged on a cross.

Even on the cross in the midst of indescribable pain He could in dignity turn to His fellow sufferer on one of the other crosses and meet his searching need; He could also have concern for His mother and her future as she agonized in bewilderment at the foot of His cross.

Every year before Easter the words of Jesus on the cross are emphasized. They really come out of His very experience of His heavenly Father. They show the final test of the authenticity of His experience of God. In the midst of the increasing physical agony He cried, *"Father, forgive them; for they know not what they do."* Evil, let loose, had done everything it could to Him; but they could get nothing out of Him but love, because that is all that was in Him. The more evil they did to Him, the more love He expressed. We have heard throughout our lives that He died for us. Here indeed He pleads for humanity. He sides with us because we just don't know what we are doing. He was truly forgiving, even to those who should have known better

118

— the ones who professed to know God but who had brought this suffering on Him. He could not hate them or wish them ill. "Father, forgive. . . ."

Jesus heard the two men talking who were crucified with Him, the one speaking in ridicule and the other rebuking him. This one, in his final hour, recognized truth and royal power in Jesus. Jesus could more than meet his need: "Truly, I say to you, today you will be with me in Paradise" (Luke 23:43). So Jesus identified with this man, the scum of the earth socially and morally.

Next Jesus turned to His suffering mother, His aunt, His beloved John, and Mary Magdalene and entered into their suffering. Seeing their suffering increased His own as He looked on them in concerned love. His mother was His prime relationship to humanity, so He asked John to care for her: "Woman, behold your son" and to John, "Behold your mother!" From that hour John did care for her.

As Jesus entered even more fully into the consciousness of man's blinding sin, He cried out, "My God, my God, why hast thou forsaken me?" This was a quotation from Psalm 22. Every Jew, I am told, knew the whole psalm, and any verse from it would be taken in its whole context. *This cry of despair and alienation is in the very context of faith in God.*

The body of His humanness cried out, "I thirst." Luke says He then cried with a loud voice, " 'Father, into thy hands I commit my spirit!' And having said this he breathed his last" (Luke 23:46). John says He added, "It is finished!" (John 19:30). This was the final statement of the humanity of the Son of God. In full confidence He turned to His heavenly Father, and He knew His ministry on earth was now finished. He did not need a voice from heaven saying God was well pleased; He was there with the Father, unhampered by the limitations of the flesh. His ministry for our redemption was complete.

The wonder of His resurrection we will see through the eyes of Peter who loved Him as his Master in the flesh and served Him with abandon and new power as his risen, living Lord.

11
PETER BEFORE PENTECOST

Simon Peter was so much like a Western activist today that we can learn much from him. He was an ordinary follower of Jesus when he was *with* Jesus; but when we look at him *after* Pentecost and see what a change the Spirit made in his life, we can take courage and hope for real changes in our own lives. He was first known as Simon — a lovable fellow, warm-hearted, loyal, often hotheaded, and frequently unstable. His friends probably smiled at his enthusiasm. He was often an impatient enthusiast and must have longed for steadfastness and poise.

It was common conversation and a common hope that a Messiah would come and free the Jewish nation from the power of Rome. Nevertheless Simon must have been surprised that morning when his brother Andrew came to him and said, "We have found the

Messiah." Andrew took Simon to Jesus. Jesus looked into his heart and said, "So you are Simon the son of John? You shall be called Cephas (which means Peter [or rock])" (John 1:42). What a surprise this was to Simon! A new name. A name to live up to! A rock was exactly what Simon wanted to be but was not!

Andrew and Peter were skilled fishermen, and one day after Peter got his new name, he was washing his nets when Jesus came along. So many people crowded around Jesus on the shore that He got into Peter's boat and began to teach the people from there. After a while Jesus asked Peter to move out into the deep and put his net down for a catch. Simon Peter, the fisherman, said to Jesus, the carpenter, "Master, we toiled all night and took nothing! But at your word I will let down the nets" (Luke 5:5). He let them down and caught so many fish his nets were breaking, and he had to call to the other fishermen for help. This man Jesus was more than a carpenter. Peter fell down on his knees before Him, confessing his own sinfulness and unworthiness. He was now conditioned to hear the call from Jesus: "Do not be afraid; henceforth you will be catching men" (5:10). When they got to land, Simon Peter and the other fishermen left everything to follow Jesus.

From there Jesus, with the four fishermen, went to Capernaum and taught in the synagogue on the Sabbath day. A demon-possessed man was present who cried out, "What have you to do with us, Jesus of Nazareth? Have you come to destroy us? I know who you are, the Holy One of God" (Mark 1:24). Jesus rebuked the evil spirit in the man, saying, "Be silent, and come out of him!'' (1:25). The man was instantly healed, and all the people were amazed.

After the service Jesus went to Simon Peter's house for dinner. Simon's mother-in-law was sick, but Jesus healed her, and she got up and served them. Then at sundown, which was the end of the Sabbath, the crowds came with their sick ones, and Jesus healed many of them. What an exciting day this was! Simon Peter had many things to think about that night: how wonderful Jesus was, how popular He was, how glad he was he had decided to follow Him! This was indeed the Messiah!

The next morning when Simon Peter awoke, rejoicing that he could have Jesus as a guest in his home, he was surprised to find Him gone. So he and his friends went in search of Jesus, and they found Him out in a lonely spot praying. They said to Him, ''Everyone is searching for you.'' Jesus answered them, ''Let us go on to the next towns, that I may preach there also; for that is why I came out'' (Mark 1:38). How strange it must have seemed to an activist like Peter not to try to cash in on Jesus' growing popularity!

There followed many miracles and much teaching and then another occasion when Jesus disappeared in the hills, this time to pray all night (Luke 6:12). The next morning He called His followers together, and from among them He chose twelve whom He named apostles. They were called ''to be with [Jesus], and to be sent out to preach and have authority to cast out demons'' (Mark 3:14,15). Those chosen were surely surprised among themselves: There was Matthew, the tax collector (of course he had already left his job to follow Jesus); Simon the Zealot, who wanted to hasten the work of the Messiah by the sword; and Judas Iscariot, the only Judean among them. How glad the four fishermen were — Andrew, Simon (now called Peter), James, and John — to be among the chosen twelve.

These twelve men were to be taught by Jesus in the style of an oriental school. They would live with their teacher and learn from His life as well as from His words. As Jesus trained them for service, they found there was no difference between what He taught and what He was. They saw His complete dedication to God, His oneness with God as heavenly Father, His love for the people, His constant compassion for the suffering and dispossessed, His infinite patience with the ''riffraff'' of their day. He seemed to feel at home with the very ones the religious leaders took special pains to avoid: He ate with the socially and politically despised tax collectors; He had no fear for His reputation when He saw spiritual hunger in the heart of a prostitute; and He even touched lepers.

These men whom Jesus called apostles must have been bewildered to the point of shock many times, but the love and dignity of Jesus held them. There was always that sense of spiritual authority in Him which they were not able to analyze. None loved Him more than the warm-hearted Peter, who could never forget the confidence Jesus had in him at their first meeting, a confidence in his own deep desire to be a better man. He really wanted to be steady and strong as *rock*. He still failed at times, but he never felt watched or policed. No committee was appointed to see if he lived up to his new name. Somehow Jesus had set him free to learn this new way of life.

One day Jesus asked the disciples to pray the Lord of the harvest to send out laborers into the harvest; then He immediately commissioned the Twelve to go out among the people and do the very works they had watched Him do. Jesus told them not to be anxious about any emergency they might meet; they would be given power to speak and to act. So they went out, preaching and healing people as they had seen Jesus do. (See Matt. 9:35–10:42; Mark 6:7-13; Luke 9:1-6.)

It must have been spiritually exciting to have this new power for preaching and healing. The disciples returned and reported the wonder of their new experiences. Jesus suggested a retreat with them, where they would have more time to talk of what they had experienced. But again there were interruptions. Couldn't they ever get away from the crowds even for a short time? The apostles' wonder grew, because Jesus always welcomed such interruptions. He indeed seemed to have unlimited love for the people, all people. Jesus took every opportunity to teach those who came to hear Him. What a story the apostles had to tell after taking part in the feeding of five thousand people *besides* women and children. No wonder the people wanted to make Jesus king. The disciples must have thought this was the hour Jesus would accept the homage of the people, but He dismissed the crowd and sent the apostles off in a boat, while He went away by Himself into the hills to pray. Simon the Zealot and impatient Peter must have wondered why the Master would ignore such opportunities for glory due Him.

The fishermen never forgot that night on the lake. The wind came up, and even these experienced sailors were distressed. Jesus saw their plight and came to them, walking on the water. They were all the more frightened because they thought He was a ghost. But Jesus said to them, "Take heart, it is I; have no fear." Peter quickly responded, "Lord, if it is you, bid me come to you on the water." And Jesus said, "Come." So Peter got out of the boat and walked on the water toward Jesus; but then he felt the wind, and he was afraid. He began to sink and cried out to Jesus, "Lord, save me." Jesus got into the boat with them and the wind ceased (Matt. 14:22-33; also Mark 6:47-52; John 6:16-21). Jesus is even more available to us through the Holy Spirit to meet us in the midst of our fears today.

After Jesus preached His sermon on the Bread of Life, many of the people turned away from Him because they wanted only physical benefits, not spiritual food. Jesus asked the Twelve, "Do you also wish to go away?" Peter answered at once, "Lord, to whom shall we go? You have the words of eternal life; and we have believed, and have come to know, that you are the Holy One of God" (John 6:67-69). Jesus was constantly meeting the physical needs of persons, but He never bargained with those He healed; He never catered to the self-centeredness of people. This was an important lesson for the disciples to learn in an authentic relationship with God.

Jesus yearned for this growing understanding in

His disciples and rejoiced at every evidence of growth. Nothing meant more to Peter than to please His Master. One day as they walked along the road, Jesus asked, "Who do men say that I am?" (Mark 8:27). After they answered for others, Jesus asked, "But who do you say that I am?" Peter was ready, "You are the Christ, the Son of the living God." Jesus answered Peter, "Blessed are you, Simon Bar-Jona! For flesh and blood has not revealed this to you, but my Father who is in heaven" (Matt. 16:15-17).

Jesus then began to tell them that He must go to Jerusalem, suffer many things, and be killed. They couldn't see that, and even less could they understand the promise of a resurrection. So Peter, somewhat puffed up from the previous praise, began to rebuke his Master. "God forbid, Lord! This shall never happen to you" (Matt. 16:23). This time Jesus rebuked Peter in the presence of the other disciples: "Get behind me, Satan! You are a hindrance to me; for you are not on the side of God but of men" (16:23). I suppose the eleven were glad they had kept their mouths shut, but none could understand Jesus' continual talk of death.

Jesus called the waiting crowd to Him and said to them, as well as to His own men, "If any man would come after me, let him deny himself and take up his cross daily and follow me. For whoever would save his life will lose it; and whoever loses his life for my sake, he will save it" (Luke 9:23,24). After the day of Pentecost Peter learned the real meaning of these words, but many of Jesus' disciples of today are still with the pre-Pentecost Peter in not understanding about death to self to reach fulfillment of life.

Jesus' teachings about servanthood and childlike humility were hard for an activist like Peter to understand, because he could not see being passive about anything important. But the servanthood that Jesus was trying to explain to them was not passive at all; it was an outgoing good will to others in forgiveness and reconciliation. Relationships with others must be maintained by establishing rapport and not by force.

Jesus suggested three steps to take to win the angered man. If all efforts fail, "Let him be to you as a Gentile and a tax collector" (Matt. 18:17). For years I thought this was the end and one could turn his back on the angered one. Then I remembered that Jesus said He did not come to save the righteous but the sinners. (We should couple Matthew 5:23,24 with this advice — in either case I must take the initiative toward reconciliation, whether my brother sinned against me or whether he says I sinned against him.) Really, Jesus said if you fail you start all over again beginning with prayer: "Again I say to you, if two of you agree on earth about anything they ask, it will be done for them by my Father in heaven. For where two or three are gathered in my name, there am I in the midst of them" (vv. 19,20).

Peter recognized that Jesus was still talking about forgiveness, so he asked, "Lord, how often shall my brother sin against me and I forgive him? As many as seven times?" Peter was really patting himself on the back for his generosity, because the rabbis interpreted the law of forgiveness to mean that a man was to forgive three times and that was enough. Peter must have been surprised when Jesus answered, "I do not say to you seven times, but seventy times seven" (v. 22). That meant to forgive endlessly. To Peter, and too often to us, that seemed impossible.

Peter did not know yet (and we too often forget) that forgiveness is even more necessary for the forgiver than for the one forgiven. When we do not forgive, our hearts are hard and closed toward God and others. I have a beautiful friend who is just now finding freedom toward God and her loving husband, because at last she has been able to forgive her mother who sinned against her as a child. Peter was to find many reasons for the need of the grace of forgiveness before much more time passed.

The news was out now that the Jews in Jerusalem wanted to kill Jesus, but He set His face to go to Jerusalem anyway. When He arrived there, efforts were made to arrest Him, but Jesus was secure in His faith in the Father's timing.

So many things were happening, and the air was so full of intrigue that Peter and the others had plenty to think about. They were in the temple on the last of the Feast of Tabernacles. During this feast, a priest would take a quart of water in a golden pitcher and pour it out on the altar to commemorate the water from the rock in the Sinai desert. Jesus was always so relevant. I can imagine Him in the midst of the people (He had no credentials to serve at the altar) as He stood up and said, "If any one thirst, let him come to me and drink. He who believes in me . . . 'Out of his heart shall flow rivers of living water' " (John 7:37,38). Many years later, after experience had verified the truth of Jesus' teaching, John explained what Jesus meant by this statement. There was a coming of the Spirit to be dated in history that would be different from any experience of any of the faithful up to that time. But the disciples did not yet understand what all this meant. Besides, they were still thinking in terms of a nation.

Life for Peter had become constant excitement. He had a deepening amazement at the power and poise of Jesus but increasing fear because of the growing intrigue against Jesus. But through it all he never questioned his own commitment to the Master. The day the rich young ruler walked away because Jesus challenged him to put God above his wealth, Peter said to Jesus, "Lo, we have left everything and followed you. What then shall we have?" (Matt. 19:27). Jesus might have rebuked him for wanting returns, but He answered graciously that he who left all for Christ would receive one-hundredfold in spiritual things.

In spite of his growing anxiety, a great sense of victory must have come to Peter on that glorious day of the triumphal entry into Jerusalem. At last Jesus was being given due honor. Surely the new day for their nation was dawning at last. Forgotten for the moment was all the news of intrigue — this time they thought they had real reason to expect victory. Jesus even got away with the cleansing of the temple. The sense of authority they had recognized in Him was now bearing fruit in Jerusalem.

But their Sunday hopes did not last long. The week following became the most intense and tragic of

130

all Peter's life. It was not so bad when the disciples were alone with Jesus, but at every opportunity He was the target of the religious authorities, who wanted to trap Him. It was one thing when the questions were Jewish questions; but when the government was involved, the nationalists and zealots would be excited and the government would be wary. So there was double tension when the Pharisees and the Herodians tried to trap Jesus. The religious people aimed to catch something from His talk that they could use against Him before the governor. They pretended sincerity, but Jesus knew their scheme.

Passover time was approaching. On Thursday of that last week Jesus sent Peter and John to prepare for their Passover meal together. They would eat it as a family a day early. At the evening hour Jesus sat at the table with the Twelve and explained how He had looked forward to this meal with them before His suffering. Jesus blessed the meal, and then to their astonishment and bewilderment, He took a towel and knelt down to wash their feet. A master could not do this! It was more than Peter could take. He exclaimed, "Lord, do you wash my feet? . . . You shall never wash my feet." Jesus answered Peter, "If I do not wash you, you have no part in me." Characteristically, Peter replied, "Lord, not my feet only but also my hands and my head!" He was ready for a full bath if that would make a difference in his relationship to the Master. After Jesus had finished washing their feet, He asked if they knew what He had done to them. But they still did not understand the role of servanthood.

Jesus told them that one of them would betray Him. They had been with Judas all this time but had never suspected him of disloyalty. Each one looked to himself, "Is it I?" Peter asked John, who was sitting next to Jesus, to ask Him who it was, and John inquired, "Who is it?" Judas also asked, "Is it I, Master?" Jesus replied, "Judas, you have said so." With all this, the others still did not suspect Judas, even when he suddenly left the room. After Judas was gone, Jesus took bread and blessed it and gave to each one, saying, "This is my body." Next he took the cup and blessed it and gave them to drink, saying, "This is my blood of the covenant, which is poured out for many for the forgiveness of sins" (Matt. 26:28).

After this ceremony Jesus told them that He was going to leave them and that they would fall away. Peter exclaimed, "Even though they all fall away, I will not." Jesus assured Peter that He had prayed for him, but added, "This very night, before the cock crows twice, you will deny me three times." This could not be. Peter answered, "Even if I must die with you, I will not deny you." I feel sure Peter meant this with his whole heart. And the rest of the disciples echoed the same loyalty.

During all Jesus' ministry up to this time His main teaching had been concerning the coming kingdom, the realm of God's rule, and the principles for living in that kingdom. Now He was going to leave them as a human Master, and He had to prepare them for His seeming absence. There was no secretary present in that meeting to take down the words of Jesus, but that does not bother me at all. In fact, it means more to me nineteen hundred years later that these words of Jesus were experienced before they were written. That night they did not understand what Jesus was talking about, so any minutes taken at the time might have been a misrepresentation. But after enlightenment and discernment through the Holy Spirit came, they could record accurately what He had taught. He was saying that the Holy Spirit, who was to come in a new way, was not a substitute for Him in His "absence," but would be the agent of His living presence. That night the disciples were *with* Jesus, but through the Holy Spirit He would be *in* them. The parable of this new relationship that He gave them was of the vine and the branches. His life would flow into them, the branches. These were all mysterious ideas to the disciples that night.

Without personal experience they are still mysterious ideas to many Christians. But if the experience is sought for itself, the "mystery" will never unfold. For the "mystery" is Christ. As we read what He said to the disciples about the Holy Spirit, we must remember that in Him we have the perfect illustration of a man baptized in the Spirit, filled with the Spirit, or whatever anyone wants to call this experience of God.

In the last chapter we went through the Garden of Gethsemane with Jesus. It is a heartbreaking experience as we think of His suffering for us. Perhaps this was a deeper suffering than the physical suffering on the cross. But Peter was still ignorant of what was really happening to his world. He was tired, and he and the

133

other two of the inner circle slept through their Master's hour of agony. Jesus came to them after His first period of prayer and found them sleeping. He said to Peter, who had boasted of his loyalty, "Simon, are you asleep? Could you not watch one hour? Watch and pray that you may enter not into temptation; the spirit indeed is willing, but the flesh is weak" (Mark 14:37,38). (How often this last statement of Jesus is quoted as an excuse for human weakness when it is really a confession of brotherhood with the old Peter, who was still ignorant spiritually.)

After His second time of prayer and again after a third time of agonizing prayer, Jesus still found them asleep. As we see it, we say, "Incredible!" This time Jesus said, "Rise, let us be going; see, my betrayer is at hand." The three closest to their Lord did not know what they had missed in not giving comfort to their beloved Master.

If Peter and the others had been wondering where Judas had gone, now they found out. There came Judas leading a crowd with swords, all sent by the priests, scribes, and elders! Judas came and kissed his Master, and then those with him laid hands on Jesus and arrested him. Peter had a sword, too. How long had he been "prepared"? Having a sword, he used it. He cut off the ear of the high priest's slave. But Jesus touched the slave's ear, healed it, and rebuked Peter for using the sword. This was not *that* kind of conflict. Peter was the type who had courage as long as he could *do* something about the situation. But when he had to wait in the midst of danger, he was paralyzed by his bewilderment. Jesus showed no fear; in fact those who came to capture Him were almost helpless for a moment before His infinite courage and authority. Finally they bound Him, and the disciples all forsook Him and fled. Peter forgot everything. Poor Peter!

It was the law in the Mishna that all proceedings involving the life of a man must take place in the full light of day, but the religious authorities could not run the risk of waiting because of their fear of the people. The Sanhedrin was summoned, and the trial began. By this time Peter had collected himself enough to follow at a distance to see what was going to happen. John also had come, and because he knew the high priest he was permitted to enter where Jesus was. John saw Peter standing outside the door, so he persuaded the maid who guarded the door to let Peter come into the court-yard. The maid said to Peter, "Are you not also one of this man's disciples?" Peter retorted, "I am not." Then he sat with the guards and warmed himself by the fire which they had kindled. The maid said to the bystanders, "This man *is* one of them." For the second time Peter denied his Lord. After about an hour the bystanders said to Peter, "Certainly you are one of them, for you are a Galilean." Peter was so frustrated by the turn of events that even after an hour he had not regained his senses. He couldn't understand how Jesus could be a powerless victim. He couldn't see through this tragedy. He was in shock.

Then the cock crowed! And Peter remembered! The realization of how he had failed his Lord began to dawn on him. Then he looked up, and Jesus turned and *looked* at him. He could not forget that *look*. We can only guess at the depth of love and sympathy in the look of the Master. Peter went out and wept bitterly.

Worse than Peter's failure, though, was the portrayal of religiosity in those who brought Jesus to trial. They were the "orthodox" religious leaders. They could not enter the Roman court lest they be ceremonially defiled for eating the Passover (John 18:28) — but they could have a good man killed!

Where did Peter go to shed his tears? We do not know. Was he on the outskirts of the crowd during all the trials, scourgings, tauntings, and horrors of that night? Was he on the outskirts of the crowd when they crucified the Lord, now feeling too unworthy to be near? Ralph Conner pictured him as going out to the city dump — Gehenna — where he felt he belonged as he faced the greatest failure of his life. Even if Jesus wasn't the one to restore the kingdom to Israel, Peter still loved Him with all his heart. Conner imagined Peter there in his despair, when he looked up suddenly and saw Judas coming toward him. He belonged in the city dump also. But Judas did not see Peter. To Peter's horror he saw Judas tie a rope around his neck, and fastening it to a tree he let himself drop over the ledge to his death. Poor Judas! Was his suicide the measure of his love for the Master and of his blasted hopes for a different kind of a kingdom? Had he really only tried to force the hand of the Master to earthly victory as *he*, Judas, saw it? Peter did not sleep that night. Where was he all day Saturday? Was he able to sleep on Saturday night with the body of his Lord in the tomb?

No one seemed to remember that Jesus had told them three times that He would suffer, die, and then be raised again on the third day. Their hopes were all blasted. The future was dark, and they could not see through the darkness. So on Sunday morning Peter was astonished almost beyond belief when the women hunted him up and cried, ''He is alive! And, Peter, he asked especially that you be told.'' Peter was overjoyed. The Master is alive! He *is* the same, the same *love,* the same *forgiveness!* Peter and John ran to the tomb and found it empty as the women had said. Would he really see Jesus alive again so he could ask forgiveness and confess his love anew? Peter could hardly wait.

Somewhere they had their reunion. The two men who met the risen Lord on the road to Emmaus reported to the disciples that night in Jerusalem about their meeting, how they had finally recognized Him, and how the Lord had also had a private meeting with Peter. Many years later Paul also told about this special meeting with Peter. Peter must have told Paul when Paul came to Jerusalem to get acquainted with him.

For the next forty days Jesus would suddenly appear in their midst. As a child I wondered how He could get through the walls when He appeared to them in the locked room, but now I know He was present all the time and only needed to make Himself visible to their physical eyes. His natural resurrected body was the unseen one; the other was an *appearance*. Anyway, they got into the habit of feeling the joy of His presence even when they could not see Him. He was alive!

Those forty days were a strange time of waiting and adjustment. No one knew what to expect next. The disciples were still overcome with surprise and joy. And waiting was still hard on Peter. One day he said, "I am going fishing." Others went with him. They toiled all night and caught nothing. Had they lost their skill? As the day was breaking, a man stood on the beach and told them to cast their net on the right side of the boat. They caught so many fish they could not haul in the net. Then John recognized Jesus. Peter jumped out and waded to shore. Jesus sent him back to get some fish for breakfast. After they had eaten, Jesus asked Peter, "Simon, son of John, do you love Me more than these?" Peter answered, "Yes, Lord; You know that I love You." Then Jesus said, "Feed My lambs." Twice more Jesus asked if he loved Him, and twice Peter vowed his love. Each time Jesus said, "Feed My sheep." Did Jesus want three avowals of love to counteract Peter's memory of his three denials?

At Jesus' last appearance with His disciples, they again asked the old question, "Lord, will you at this time restore the kingdom to Israel?" (Acts 1:6). How hard it is to change one's theology! Jesus told them the old political issue was not their concern — "But you shall receive power when the Holy Spirit has come upon you; and you shall be my witnesses in Jerusalem and in all Judea and Samaria and to the end of the earth" (1:8).

Jesus added, "Stay in the city until you are clothed with power from on high" (Luke 24:49). Then a cloud

138

took Jesus out of their sight, and two men stood by them in white robes and said, "Why do you stand looking into heaven? This Jesus, who was taken up from you into heaven, will come in the same way as you saw him go into heaven" (Acts 1:11).

When Jesus disappeared from them in death, they were in abject despair, but when He disappeared from their sight this time, they were full of joy. In that joy they returned to Jerusalem to wait for whatever was going to happen. They did not know what was coming, but they knew the Lord who had made them a promise. They knew He was alive, and they would worship while they waited. There were 120 who waited in an upper room. Jesus' mother was there, and at last His own brothers joined the group of waiting disciples. While waiting, they devoted themselves to prayer. Of course the Eleven were there.

And so ten days were passed in prayerful waiting. They did not yet know what to expect, but they believed the promise of Jesus. So they waited in joy.

Jesus was alive!

12
PETER AFTER PENTECOST

Joy is an attitude of faith. With joy, there is no fear that anything will go wrong. In that upper room the disciples waited *without striving for any personal experience*. They were filled with dynamic peace because they believed the promise Jesus had made them, and they waited in obedience for the promise to be fulfilled. While waiting, they chose another to take the place of Judas. Many thoughts must have gone through their minds during those days. Did Peter in his own heart come to the place where he eschewed all self-striving? Did he yield his impulsiveness as well as his love to the risen Lord? Did James and John give up all their desires for first place in the kingdom? Did Thomas give over all his doubts? A new humility must have grown in their waiting hearts. They were growing in their own attitude of faith to the place where God *could* come to them with the new promised power. It takes preparation to handle power.

The day of Pentecost was a Jewish holiday. There is always an air of expectancy before a big holiday. On this day, for the followers of Jesus, there was a double expectancy. Then it happened! A sound from heaven filled the house; a tongue of fire appeared on the head of each person present; they were all filled with the Holy Spirit and began to speak as the Spirit gave them utterance. The sound was so great the multitude outside heard it and came together, and to their amazement each one heard the disciples speaking in his own language. This was a miracle in communication, for people were in Jerusalem from many language areas.

Peter was still the ready spokesman. But this time he got up *with the others,* not in competition with them. He preached the first sermon of the Christian church. He quoted the prophecy of Joel concerning the promise of the Spirit (Joel 2:28-32), and he said with assurance, "This is it." They just *knew.*

Peter could now talk of Christ's death and resurrection with an understanding he never had when the Lord was with them in the flesh. "Let all the house of Israel therefore know assuredly that God has made him both Lord and Christ, this Jesus whom you crucified" (Acts 2:36). This courageous statement was made by the same, and yet not the same, Peter who less than two months before had denied any relationship with Jesus before a servant girl!

Jesus had told the disciples on that last night that when the Holy Spirit came He would bring conviction

141

of sin (John 16:8). Most of our failures come when we usurp the work of the Spirit and try ourselves to bring conviction to people. The people cried out, "What shall we do?" Now Peter knew. He said, "Repent, and be baptized every one of you in the name of Jesus Christ for the forgiveness of your sins; and you shall receive the gift of the Holy Spirit. For the promise is to you and to your children and to all that are far off, every one whom the Lord our God calls to him" (Acts 2:38,39).

Peter saw what many Christians today do not realize — that this gift of the Holy Spirit is a norm in the experience of a Christian. It was not for the apostles only, or for the people in the upper room only, or for the people of that day only, but for all of us who love the Lord Jesus Christ. It is tragic when we do not accept the gift of God waiting for us.

To know what really happened on the day of Pentecost one must read more than the second chapter of Acts. The outward evidences in that room that day were minor compared to the power released in the lives of otherwise insignificant people. The outward evidences were a joy to experience and remember, but the new consciousness of the presence of Christ in their lives was so wonderful that they understood now what He meant when He said it was better for Him to leave them so the Spirit could come. It took the whole Book of Acts to tell what happened that day, as well as the letters of the New Testament. If you want to know about that great day, read the whole Book of Acts — in one sitting.

Three thousand people were added to their number

on that day, and after this, "The Lord added to their number day by day those who were being saved" (Acts 2:47). Holy Spirit evangelism was more efficient than all our modern committee planning. It is true, organization is needed, but it can never be a substitute for the work of the Spirit.

The disciples were now living on a new plane of consciousness. There was a naturalism in the new power. They were more conscious of this power than they were of themselves. They continued to go to the temple to worship but had separate meetings also among themselves. They sold what they owned and had all things in common. You see, they had a new love for one another and *wanted* to share together.

One day Peter and John were going up to the temple at the hour of prayer. A lame man, who was carried there daily so that he might beg from the worshipers, asked them for money. They must have seen this man often. Undoubtedly, they had given alms to him. But this day, as naturally as breathing, Peter looked at the man and said, "I have no silver and gold, but I give you what I have; in the name of Jesus Christ of Nazareth, walk" (3:6). Then Peter took the man by the hand and raised him up, and immediately he was healed. The man went into the temple with Peter and John. Peter had said to him, "Look at us," and he did, but after being healed he praised God, not Peter and John. It is when we go beyond what our education and training warrant that people begin to wonder about the source of the extra power.

This man clung to Peter and John, and the people

143

crowded around. So Peter preached another sermon. He asked why they stared at them as though by their own piety or power they had made this man walk. He said it was Jesus whom they had crucified who had healed the man. Then Peter showed a magnanimity unknown to him in the old days. He said, "I know that you acted in ignorance, as did also your rulers" (3:17). Then Peter called on the people to repent and believe on the risen Lord. By not being vindictive Peter made it easier for the people to believe in Jesus. Many of the people did believe, and the number of Christians came now to five thousand.

The religious authorities, including the Sadducees, were much annoyed because Peter and John were proclaiming Jesus' resurrection from the dead, and they came and arrested them and put them into custody. The next morning all the religious authorities were there when Peter and John were brought before them. And they set a trap for themselves when they asked, "By what power or by what name did you do this?" Then Peter, "filled with the Holy Spirit" and no longer afraid, said, " 'Be it known to you all . . . that by the name of Jesus Christ of Nazareth, whom you crucified, whom God raised from the dead, by him this man is standing before you well.' . . . Now when they saw the boldness of Peter and John, and perceived that they were uneducated, common men, they wondered; and they recognized that they had been with Jesus" (4:10,13).

Seeing the healed man standing with them, the authorities could not speak in opposition to Peter and

John. They sent them out of the council room and then discussed how to keep the two from speaking in the name of Jesus. That was a real problem with such evidence walking around. All they could do was warn and threaten them. But the warnings had no effect on Peter and John. They answered these men who thought they represented God in Israel: "Whether it is right in the sight of God to listen to you rather than to God, you must judge; for we cannot but speak of what we have seen and heard" (4:19,20).

Once released they went to their Christian friends and reported all that had happened to them. When they heard it, they spontaneously turned to God in prayer. This prayer meeting was not the kind many churches have every week. It was the kind that made history. They began by expressing God's greatness and how they could trust Him. It looked as if the ones who had crucified Jesus were now on their tracks, and they realized that they must be ready for anything that might happen to them. They asked for boldness, not protection (4:29,30).

No wonder the place was shaken and they were conscious of greater infilling of the Holy Spirit.

One might think that the group of 120 would be swallowed up in the thousands more who joined them, but the power in their midst was great enough to encompass all. They felt no need — yet — to appoint a committee to work out a socio-economic plan whereby they might live according to the principles of Jesus. They loved each other and the Lord, and they *wanted* to share with one another. Spontaneously those who had

145

land and possessions sold all they had and put the proceeds into the common fund. There were to be no rich and no poor among them. They would be one in Christ. No orders had been given nor rules made. This community living was not the main miracle; it was merely a method. The miracle was that the company of those who believed were of one heart and soul.

Ananias and Sapphira were a couple among them who wanted credit for having given all the proceeds to the common fund from selling their property, but they kept some of the money to use for themselves. When Ananias brought his part of the money to the apostles, Peter immediately discerned the deception. He did not chide Ananias for keeping part of the money; rather, he said, "Ananias, why has Satan filled your heart to lie to the Holy Spirit and to keep back part of the proceeds of the land? While it remained unsold, did it not remain your own? And after it was sold, was it not at your disposal? . . . You have not lied to men but to God" (5:3,4). Peter saw a sin deeper than stealing — the sin of spiritual pride. When Ananias realized that he had sinned against God in this deception, he fell over dead.

In about three hours Sapphira came in with her gift, telling the same story, and Peter said to her, "How is it that you have agreed together to tempt the Spirit of the Lord? Hark, the feet of those that have buried your husband are at the door and they will carry you out" (v. 9). So she was buried beside her husband. So strong was the power of the Spirit in the fellowship that to sin against fellow believers and God shocked the couple into heart failure.

146

Peter, being spokesman, was evidently looked to as leader both in speaking and healing, "so that they even carried out the sick into the streets, and laid them on beds and pallets, that as Peter came by at least his shadow might fall on some of them" (v. 15). The old Peter would have been inflated by this honor, but the Spirit-filled Peter was so full of awe at the work of the Spirit that he walked in humility.

The authorities grew angry again in their jealousy, and so the apostles were arrested and put in the common prison. They got out that night, released by an angel, but they didn't hide. Instead they returned to the temple at daybreak to continue their preaching. The council met to try the men and sent to the prison for them, but they were not there. Then someone came and said the men were in the temple teaching the people! There is no one so helpless as the man in a place of power who cannot frighten people with his power. The high priest said to them, "We strictly charged you not to teach in this name, yet here you have filled Jerusalem with your teaching" (v. 28). Peter could only answer, "We must obey God rather than men" (v. 29). The religious authorities were enraged and wanted to kill them. But there was one man in the council who had wisdom. He said, "Take care what you do with these men. . . . for if this plan or this undertaking is of men, it will fail; but if it is of God, you will not be able to overthrow them. You might even be found opposing God!" (vv. 35,38,39). Gamaliel's word prevailed.

However, the authorities had the men beaten, charged them not to preach, and let them go. "Then they left the presence of the council, rejoicing that they were counted worthy to suffer dishonor for the name. And every day in the temple and at home they did not cease teaching and preaching Jesus as the Christ" (vv. 41,42).

With the phenomenal increase in the number of Christians, the need for some organization became apparent. The Jewish Christians of Grecian background, the Hellenists, complained because their widows were neglected in the daily distribution. The Twelve called the body of disciples together and said, "It is not right that we should give up preaching the word of God to serve tables. Therefore, brethren, pick out from among you seven men of good repute, full of the Spirit and of wisdom, whom we may appoint to this duty. But we will devote ourselves to prayer and to the ministry of the word" (6:2-4). This pleased the people, and none saw anything wrong in this division of labor. At least they recognized that even "serving tables" required the power of the Spirit. The men of prayer and preaching had no exclusive rights to the work of the Spirit. So they chose seven men full of faith and of the Holy Spirit to care for the distribution of food and other necessities.

Through the years I have heard even famous preachers say that the apostles made a mistake in this division of service. Be that as it may, the wonder is that they were never bound by this first effort at organization. One never knows what will happen when the Spirit is in control! The Twelve were amenable to changing conditions and entirely responsive to the

148

guidance of the Spirit. Two of the appointed deacons became great preachers. Stephen was the first Christian martyr, and Philip became such a great evangelist that for the rest of his life he was known as ''Philip the Evangelist.'' Philip even had four daughters who were preachers! The remarkable fact in all this was that Peter and the other apostles never applied the brakes to the deacons for preaching. They didn't say, ''We are the preachers, and we laid hands on you to dedicate you for serving work.''

When the apostles at Jerusalem heard of Philip's great results in meetings in Samaria, they sent Peter and John to him. The people had been baptized only (by a deacon?) and had not yet received the baptism of the Holy Spirit. So Peter and John prayed for the people to receive the Spirit, and they were filled with the Spirit.

There was a famous magician named Simon who had also become a convert. When Simon saw that the Spirit came with the laying on of hands, he wanted the same ability to pray for people to receive the Spirit. Doesn't that sound like a laudable request? But he offered money for the gift! Simon the magician thought money could buy anything. It sounds like my cousin Caleb when he was two years of age. He was taken along to market and then to a nearby camp meeting. A few days later he was overheard to call out in his play, ''Holy Ghost, ten cents a pint!''

Peter knew better. He said to Simon, ''Your silver perish with you, because you thought you could obtain the gift of God with money'' (8:20). Simon then asked Peter to pray for him.

149

Peter continued his own works with great response from the people. Reports of his ministry of healing spread to many places. Eventually he came to Joppa and stayed for some time with Simon, a tanner. While he was there, the Holy Spirit was working to bring together a spiritually hungry man and the man who could help him. At Caesarea there was a centurion, a Roman officer, of the occupying army in Israel who was a devout man. He was one of many Gentiles who honored the Jewish faith, prayed to God, and gave liberally to the people. This man, Cornelius, was told by an angel in a vision that his prayers had been heard and that he was to send for one Simon who was called Peter. He was even given Peter's Joppa address. So Cornelius called three of his men and told them what had happened to him. And he sent them to Joppa to bring Peter to him.

Cornelius and his men had reason for concern. Would Peter, a Jew, come to him, a Gentile? Even the God-fearing Gentiles knew the deep prejudices the devout Jews held in regard to Gentiles. All the Gentile Christians were Jewish proselytes, and Peter had not yet faced the possibility of a Gentile becoming a Christian without *first* becoming a Jew. Of course it was a step in this direction for him to stay with a tanner, because this was an unclean job. Would God have difficulty in guiding Peter through the Holy Spirit so that he would be ready to meet the three Gentile men God was sending to him? Breaking cultural patterns is a slow process and can be a traumatic experience.

The three servants had forty miles to travel. Over

every mile they must have wondered if Peter would come with them to see their beloved master.

In the meantime, God was getting Peter ready for them. Peter had come into the house hungry. While the food was being prepared, he did what he loved to do; he went up on the housetop alone to pray. Then he got drowsy and fell into a trance and saw a sheet let down from heaven. In it were all kinds of animals which a Jew was not permitted to eat. A voice said to Peter, "Rise, Peter; kill and eat." But Peter answered, "No, Lord, for I have never eaten anything that is common or unclean." The vision was repeated, and the voice said, "What God has cleansed, you must not call common." Then it happened a third time. Peter was inwardly perplexed as to what all this might mean.

Meanwhile the men from Cornelius arrived at the door downstairs and inquired for Peter. "While Peter was pondering the vision, the Spirit said to him, 'Behold, three men are looking for you. Rise and go down, and accompany them without hesitation; for I have sent them'" (10:19,20). Of course, Peter did not know yet that the visitors were Gentiles. He went down to the men, but he was not shocked when he saw who they were because he was still *more conscious* of the Lord's will and guidance. As soon as he saw them, he said most graciously, dispelling their fears, "I am the one you are looking for; what is the reason for your coming?" (v. 21). They told the story of Cornelius and their mission.

Peter had never had Gentiles as guests before, but he called the men in for the night, a real breakthrough in

151

race relations. The next morning he went with the men, accompanied by some of the brethren. On the following day they arrived in Caesarea.

Cornelius was expecting them. He had invited relatives and close friends to be with him. Now Cornelius did not know Peter, but to him any man introduced by an angel must be great, so he bowed down to worship him. Peter lifted him up and said, "Stand up; I too am a man" (v. 26). As Peter entered the room where the guests were waiting, he dispelled any questions they might have because he was a Jew and made it easy for them to tell their story.

Cornelius told the story of his experience four days earlier and added, "So I sent to you at once, and you have been kind enough to come. Now therefore we are all here present in the sight of God, to hear all that you have been commanded by the Lord" (v. 33). What an audience to tell the Good News to! Peter told the story of Jesus' life, death, resurrection, and His command to His disciples to witness for Him. "While Peter was still saying this, the Holy Spirit fell on all who heard the word. And the believers from among the circumcised who came with Peter were amazed, because the gift of the Holy Spirit had been poured out even on the Gentiles. For they heard them speaking in tongues and extolling God" (vv. 44-46). Peter declared, "Can any one forbid water for baptizing these people who have received the Holy Spirit just as we have?" (v. 47). So they were all baptized in the name of Jesus.

When Peter and the brethren returned to the home

church in Jerusalem, they found the news about the new converts had preceded them; and the most conservative among the brethren criticized Peter for going to the Gentiles: "Why did you go to the uncircumcised men and eat with them?" (11:3). You see, they were still going by Jewish rules and didn't know any better. Peter explained everything that had happened, especially why he was sure he had followed the guidance of the Spirit; then he added, "Who was I that I could withstand God?" (v. 17). This silenced the critics and even they glorified God saying, "Then to the Gentiles also God has granted repentance unto life" (v. 18).

After the stoning of Stephen, a brilliant scholar named Saul led a persecution against the Christians and they were scattered abroad, but wherever they went they witnessed to the Lord. Then the astounding news came that Saul had become a Christian also and was preaching Christ everywhere. But apart from Saul another persecution broke out in Jerusalem. King Herod murdered James, the brother of John; and when he saw that it pleased some of the Jews, he arrested Peter also and put him in chains. Christians met at the house of Mary, mother of Mark, to pray for Peter, but they couldn't believe it when Peter appeared at their door, for an angel had released him from jail!

As the work of Saul (now Paul) progressed, some of the extreme conservatives followed his work and made trouble by telling the people that they could not be saved unless they followed the laws of Moses also. So Paul and another disciple named Barnabas were sent to the first church at Jerusalem to have this matter settled.

Again Peter had to tell how he was used of the Spirit to open the door to the Gentiles so that they could become Christians without first becoming Jews.

Before this time Paul had come to Jerusalem to visit Peter for fifteen days. If only we had a recording of their sharing together! (Gal. 1:18). But Peter's sense of responsibility to the growing conservative element in the Jerusalem church hindered him when he visited the church at Antioch. He did all right at first; he ate with the Gentiles who had become Christian. But when some of the conservative, hidebound brethren came to Antioch, Peter separated himself and ceased to eat with the Gentiles. Paul challenged him to his face before them all and talked about the wonderful grace of God and what it means to live by faith (Gal. 2). Peter evidently felt no ill will toward Paul, and he must have accepted the rebuke as from the Lord, for he later spoke of Paul as "our beloved brother" (2 Peter 3:15).

Even with this need for rebuke, Peter's life after Pentecost was miraculously different from his life before, even though then he had been *with* the Master daily. Peter loved the Lord, but that was not enough. He had to have a new power *inside* him, and that came on the day of Pentecost. Subsequently he lived in a new dimension, in the consciousness of Christ now dwelling in his life.

Many of the words of 1 and 2 Peter are appropriate to his experience and witness: "His divine power has granted to us all things that pertain to life and godliness . . . and become partakers of the divine nature. . . . For if these things are yours and abound, they keep you from being ineffective or unfruitful in the knowledge of our Lord Jesus Christ. . . . Therefore, brethren, be the more zealous to confirm your call and election, for if you do this you will never fall'' (2 Peter 1:3,4,10). That sounds like the Peter who was always falling before Pentecost and who after Pentecost found new life and power in Christ through the Holy Spirit.

Tradition says that after many fruitful years of leadership in the Jerusalem church Peter traveled far and wide and endured much suffering for the Lord, and that he was crucified in Rome by Nero. Feeling unworthy to be crucified as his Lord had been, the story goes, he requested to be crucified upside down. In the old days he had vowed he would gladly die for his Master. He did not understand the vow when he made it, but he learned its true meaning as he both lived and died for the One he loved more than his own life.

13
PAUL, THE MAN IN CHRIST

After the day of Pentecost those who had known Jesus in the flesh talked about the Holy Spirit as the source of their new power for living and service. Paul never knew Jesus as a man but met Him as the risen Lord, so he talked about being *in Christ*. Many scholars say that Paul brought a different gospel from that which Jesus had proclaimed, but the main difference was in the new relationship to Jesus as risen Lord. As Archibald Hunter has said, "Theologically, Christ and the Spirit are distinguishable; experientially, they are one."[1] So we need never stumble over a change of vocabulary from the teachings of Jesus to the letters of Peter and Paul.

A difference in vocabulary continues to this day. Those of the holiness tradition use a certain vocabulary; those of the Pentecostal background use another;

Lutherans, Presbyterians, Baptists, Catholics, and others use whatever words they understand — but when Christians get together to share in depth, somehow they *know* each other in the Spirit.

Putting into words what an experience of God means is called *theology*. When a person begins with the experience of God, it is one thing; but when one begins with theology without the experience, the spiritual life may become cold and divisive.

Since this experience of the Spirit (of Christ) is the norm for all who give themselves in complete commitment to the Lord, the experience even comes to those who know no doctrine or theology of the Spirit. I am a witness to that.

Paul is a help to us in our era because he came to the Lord *after* Pentecost. Like us, he did not know Jesus in the flesh. He had no corner on life in Christ. Whatever experience he had of the Holy Spirit, of Christ, is also available to each one of us. Unfortunately, too many Christians are living as if Pentecost never happened and even as if Jesus never came. It is important to know our true heritage in Christ. Seeing Peter before and after Pentecost is a great challenge, but Paul leaves no excuse — he is of our time.

Perhaps the most important thing about Paul was that he was completely dedicated to God before he ever knew the Lord Jesus Christ. His home nurtured him in this dedication. His parents were devout. Paul was reared a "Hebrew born of Hebrews" (Phil. 3:5). This meant careful religious training in the synagogue as well as in the home. He grew up in Tarsus, "no mean

157

city'' (Acts 21:39), in the midst of Hellenic civilization at its best and worst. Tarsus was on an important trade route. It was also an intellectual center second only to Athens and Alexandria. Paul's father was a Roman citizen as well as a citizen of Tarsus, so Paul was born to this privilege also. In other words, Paul was a citizen of two worlds: a Jew of high standing and a privileged man in the Roman Empire. But he was always grateful that he was born a Jew, and in the midst of Greek culture he was an uncompromising Jew. His leanings were toward Jerusalem rather than Rome.

He was also a devout Pharisee. As a young man he went to Jerusalem to study under the famous, wise Pharisaic rabbi, Gamaliel. A good Pharisee rendered a real service in explaining the Mosaic law so that the people would know how to be faithful. Righteousness was the main emphasis and honoring God the daily theme. So zealous was Paul, Gunther Bornkamm suggests, that he planned to be a missionary to the Gentiles, making proselytes to Judaism, even before he became a Christian.[2] Saul was his Hebrew name and Paul his Greek name. To Jews he was Saul; to the Gentiles he was Paul.

Including his Jewish background, Paul could honestly say years later that he had lived his whole life ''in all good conscience'' (Acts 23:1; see also, 24:16; 26:19). The very fact that he was so honest and faithful in following God, as his conscience dictated, created the greatest spiritual problem of his ''Jewish days.'' How could he be faithful to all the laws and traditions which he had learned as a Pharisee? *Pharisaic* tradition elaborated *360 prohibitions* and *248 commandments*. There were 1,521 Sabbath rules. And failure in one point made one guilty in all points. No wonder Paul could cry out years later, ''Wretched man that I am! Who will deliver me from this body of death?'' (Rom. 7:24). He did not know how miserable he had been until he knew the way out through Jesus Christ.

Perhaps this very sense of guilt drove him to his frenzy in persecuting the ''unorthodox'' Jews who said that Jesus was the Messiah. How could a man who had died on the cross be their Messiah? Saul watched and consented to the stoning of Stephen, and this spurred him on. ''Saul was ravaging the church, and entering house after house, he dragged off men and women and committed them to prison'' (Acts 8:3). ''But Saul, still breathing threats and murder against the disciples of the Lord, went to the high priest and asked him for letters to the synagogues at Damascus, so that if he found any belonging to the Way, men or women, he might bring them bound to Jerusalem'' (Acts 9:1,2).

The journey to Damascus, one hundred and fifty miles away, was a seven-day journey. Saul had plenty of time to think. Was he remembering Stephen's face and prayer as he died? Was Saul able to forget the grace and courage of all the others he had arrested?

Now Saul was sure these people of ''the Way'' were in the wrong. He believed they were straying from the orthodox faith. He wanted more than anything else to do God's will. Saul needed no challenge to a commitment to God. So, how could God get across to this honest, conscientious man that Jesus was truly His

159

Son? Often God has more trouble with people who have their theology "correct" than with out-and-out sinners. Argument would not do. But God found a way.

Saul thought he was obedient to God, but Jesus was not included in his theology. God had to knock him down to wake him up. As Saul neared Damascus, suddenly a great light shone upon him, and he fell to the ground. The Lord appeared to him, and a voice said, "Saul, Saul, why do you persecute me?" Saul cried, "Who are you, Lord?" The voice came back, "I am Jesus, whom you are persecuting; but rise and enter the city, and you will be told what you are to do" (9:4-6). Saul got up and discovered that he was blind. The men traveling with him had to take him by the hand and lead him into the city. So the conquering persecutor entered the city conquered by the very One he had disdained. For three days he was blind and ate no food. I'm sure he had much to think about.

But the Lord of love knew what was happening to this stormy, great-hearted man. The Lord came to Ananias in a vision and said, "Rise and go to the street called Straight, and inquire in the house of Judas for a man of Tarsus named Saul; for behold, he is praying, and he has seen a man named Ananias come in and lay his hands on him so that he might regain his sight" (9:11,12). Now, Ananias knew only too well that Saul had come to Damascus to arrest the Christians. Possibly he himself was at the head of the list. Would it be safe for him to go to Saul? But the Lord said, "Go, for he is a chosen instrument of mine to carry my name before the Gentiles and kings and the sons of Israel; for

160

I will show him how much he must suffer for the sake of my name" (vv. 15,16). So Ananias left and entered the house where Paul was; and laying his hands on Paul, he said, " 'Brother Saul, the Lord Jesus who appeared to you on the road by which you came, has sent me that you might regain your sight and be filled with the Holy Spirit.' And immediately something like scales fell from his eyes and he regained his sight. Then he rose and was baptized, and took food and was strengthened" (vv. 17-19). (See also 22:6-15; 26:4-19; Gal. 1:11-18.)

At once Saul began to preach Christ as the Son of God. He dumbfounded the Jews in Damascus, and the Christians could hardly believe that this was the man they had been told to fear.

This was such a cataclysmic experience in Saul's life that he had to think through what exactly had happened to him, so he went away into Arabia, possibly to the northern tip of that country east of Damascus. What really had happened to him?

James Stewart writes,

That Jesus Christ, whose name he had maligned, whose followers he had harried, whose cause he had striven to bring down to destruction, should nevertheless have come to meet him, and to lay his hands upon him, was a thought at once gloriously uplifting and terribly subduing. . . . And never for a moment did he doubt that the love that had come seeking him was the love of God himself. . . . All his feverish quest for peace and right-eousness and certainty was now over, for God in

Christ had taken the initiative. . . . The cataclysm of that hour ushered Paul into a totally different sphere of being. He was now as unlike the man who had set out from Jerusalem as noonday is unlike midnight, as life is unlike death. His outlook, his world, his moral sense of life – purpose – all were changed. He was a man in Christ.[3]

And Paul Tournier says that Paul was now ready to learn that

Christianity is not one ideology over against other ideologies. It is a life inspired by the Holy Spirit. Its victories are nothing but victories over itself, not over others. It propagates itself through humility and self-examination, not through triumphs.[4]

Paul's own explanation of the experience that began for him in that first encounter with the risen Lord is in his prayer for other Christians: "For this reason I bow my knees before the Father . . . that . . . he may grant you to be strengthened with might *through his Spirit* in the *inner man, and that Christ may dwell in your hearts through faith;* that you, being rooted and grounded in love, may have power to comprehend with all the saints what is the breadth and length and height and depth, and to know the love of Christ which surpasses knowledge, that you may be *filled with all the fulness of God"* (Eph. 3:14,16-19).[5]

If the unconscious, our inmost soul, is the creative area of our being, and the Holy Spirit is the creative Spirit of God whose main activity is in the unconscious, then this is the deepest kind of relationship: His Spirit in

162

the inner man, Christ in our hearts, filled with the fullness of God. This is truly experiencing God in our lives.

The work of the Holy Spirit deep in one's soul means that the basic work of the Holy Spirit is *quiet*. This is what Paul meant when he said, "If any one is in Christ, he is a new creation" (2 Cor. 5:17). The new life and the new power were amazingly *natural* to the new people. Jesus had said to His disciples, "I am with you; I will be in you." So the baptism of the Holy Spirit is the personality of Christ coming into one's innermost being to take up His abode there. This experience was the greatest theme throughout Paul's ministry. He spoke of "Christ in me" in one way or another over 160 times, and he mentioned the Holy Spirit over 100 times in his writing.

An experience of God cannot be truly analyzed. Many scholars have tried to determine just what Paul saw and heard on the Damascus road. They compare Luke's account in Acts with Paul's account in his letters and seem bewildered. The secret is not in the details; rather, it is in the fact of the encounter with the risen Lord and the real change that came into Paul's life. When an experience like this happens to anyone, he does not even need another such experience.

Paul set his experience in line with the resurrection experience of the first disciples. He stressed the fact that his experience was as real and as objective as theirs.

Still, Paul's witness never focused on his experience but on his experience of *Christ*. Paul never defended himself, only his ministry which had been given to him by the Lord. He was heartbroken whenever self-centered preachers came along in his absence from a church and confused his converts. His "boasts" were made according to what his babes in Christ had been responding to when they were manipulated by his rivals, and they were really to bring the people back to Christ as central in their lives (2 Cor. 1:10-12).

Meeting the same competition in the Philippian church, Paul added to his "boasts" (Phil. 3:8-11).

One of the greatest dangers that follows the ecstasy or joy of an experience of the Lord is that one may feel he has "arrived" when actually he has only started. This perversion of assurance in the Lord can turn any spiritual movement into a fad. The youth are so right in starting with Jesus and in emphasizing their allegiance to Him, but they must keep on growing *in* Him. So must we all, no matter how far along we think we are in the Christian life.

For one who had been so vehement against Christ, Paul's word picture of the wonder of Him is all the more remarkable.

> *He is the image of the invisible God, the first-born of all creation; for in him all things were created. . . . in him all things hold together. He is the head of the body, the church. . . . For in him all the fulness of God was pleased to dwell, . . . making peace by the blood of his cross. And you . . . he has now reconciled in his body of flesh by his death, in order to present you holy and blameless and irreproachable before him, provided that you continue in the faith (Col. 1:15-23).*

The word *provided* is so important here. We can never rest on an initial experience; we only start with it.

For himself Paul saw this clearly. He said,

> *I do not consider myself to have "arrived," spiritually, nor do I consider myself already perfect. But I keep on going, grasping ever more firmly that purpose for which Christ Jesus grasped me. My brothers, I do not consider myself to have fully grasped it even now. But I do concentrate on this: I leave the past behind and with hands outstretched to whatever lies ahead I go straight for the goal — my reward the honour of my high calling by God in Christ. All of us who are spiritually adult should set ourselves this sort of ambition, and if at present you cannot see this, yet you will find that this is the attitude which God is leading you to adopt. It is important that we go forward in the light of such truth as we have ourselves attained to (Phil. 3:12-16 Phillips).*

Paul knew that the Christ who dwelt in him through the Holy Spirit was perfect, but he also knew that he, Paul, was only in the process of being perfected. One man trained and converted under a certain "holiness doctrine" said he was perfect because the Perfect was in him. We all knew that his life was totally changed, but we also knew that he was not yet perfect. After eight months he said to me in despair, "You know, I am not perfect after all!" And I said, "Thank God, now you are in the place where you can really grow in the Lord."

Paul's phrase, "*straining* forward to what lies

ahead'' (RSV), is often misinterpreted. Paul was picturing an athletic race. He was not talking about a debilitating tension that incapacitates a person, but strict, relentless discipline, the kind that sets an athlete *free,* the kind that sets a musician *free.* A man is not ready for a real race unless he has practiced enough to have this kind of freedom. It also means that Paul was looking forward to Christ's will for him, and he pressed on no matter what happened. As we go along, God will show us where we are still short of perfection; but we should hold to what we have already attained. That is, if we are as far as high school, we should not slip back to kindergarten in the school of Christian living.

In Paul's experience this picture of disciplined freedom is balanced by his joy and peace in the Lord. ''The Lord is at hand. Have no anxiety about anything. . . . And the peace of God, which passes all understanding, will keep your hearts and your minds in Christ Jesus. . . . I have learned, in whatever state I am, to be content. . . . I can do all things in him who strengthens me'' (Phil. 4:5-7,11,13).

To the Galatians who had been ''bewitched'' into the old ways of legalism, even though in Christian terms, he wrote, ''I have been crucified with Christ; it is no longer I who live, but Christ who lives in me; and the life I now live in the flesh I live by faith in the Son of God, who loved me and gave himself for me'' (Gal. 2:20). ''For freedom Christ has set us free; stand fast therefore, and do not submit again to a yoke of slavery'' (5:1). Paul had found that the way to get out of an old legalistic attitude was through the Spirit. He pictured himself as under the law when in his own strength spiritual progress seemed so futile (Rom. 7:13-25). In such a condition he cried out, "Wretched man that I am! Who will deliver me from this body of death?" (v. 24). But he knew the answer to that cry. "Thanks be to God through Jesus Christ our Lord! . . . There is therefore no condemnation for those who are in Christ Jesus. For the law of the Spirit of life in Christ Jesus has set me free from the law of sin and death" (Rom. 7:25–8:1,2).

Belief in the indwelling Christ makes possible a full faith in the daily redeeming grace of the work of the Holy Spirit in one's life. There is real freedom in such faith. We are free to grow, and this process of growth is called sanctification. It is the unfolding of Christ's own character in the life of the one truly given to God. The changed character and disposition are fruits of the union with Christ. "But the fruit of the Spirit is love, joy, peace, patience, kindness, goodness, faithfulness, gentleness, self-control" (Gal. 5:22).

Before Paul knew the risen Lord he had no love for those who disagreed with him, he had no patience or gentleness, and he most likely justified himself in these harsh attitudes. He knew he had no goodness even though he lived in all good conscience. He had no joy or peace until he accepted the way of grace through the Holy Spirit. The *self-control* he mentions is a Greek word for *power* with the prefix *put in*. It is the Holy Spirit power put in one's heart that makes the new creature and helps him to grow. (The Greek word for self-control is the one from which we get *democracy*, people-power.)

Paul once said to the Philippians, "Work out your own salvation with fear and trembling; *for God is at work in you,* both to will and to work for his good pleasure" (Phil. 2:12,13). Seriously and reverently Paul had learned his own responsibility in permitting the grace of God to be worked out in his life.

To the Colossians Paul spelled out the process of man's part in the new life. He knew that God never overrides the human will, but that man remains responsible for his choices. "If then you have been raised with Christ, *seek* the things that are above. . . . *Set your minds* on things that are above, not on things that are on earth. For you have died, and your life is hid with Christ in God" (Col. 3:1-3). To Paul the "things that are above" were not any "pie in the sky" business but very much the business of everyday life.

He listed the things to be put to death — what one chooses against: immorality, impurity, passion, evil desire, and covetousness which is idolatry; then he made a second list which goes deeper: anger, wrath, malice, slander, lying to one another, and racial prejudice. Then a list of things to *put on:* compassion, kindness, lowliness, meekness, patience, forgiveness, and love. These are indeed the "fruit of the Spirit," but still the choice remains with the person — to grow or not to grow.

The things to be put to death are what some psychologists and psychiatrists call the *seeming* or *pseudo self.* The things that are to be put on are of the *real self.* "The real self is the alive, unique, personal center of ourselves; the only part that can, and wants to grow. The pseudo self is the slave of his own 'pride system.'"[6]

Dr. Fritz Kunkel said, "Only a single-minded person can grow; all divided minds go astray, suffer and perish, at first inwardly and then outwardly. That is not a moral law, it is a simple and inexorable biological fact. If we do not use our margin of free choice, we shall be pushed by circumstances in the wrong direction. To avoid the conscious decision is an unconscious decision in favor of destruction. We had better take the risk, therefore, consciously and deliberately."[7]

Paul's single-mindedness was in Christ: "Whatever you do, in word or deed, do everything in the name of the Lord Jesus, giving thanks to God the Father through him" (Col. 3:17).

Sometimes a "testimony meeting" sounds like a "Can you top this?" story time. With the Corinthians Paul could have topped them all, but he did not tell his more spectacular experiences until he was pushed to it *for their sakes* (2 Cor. 12:1-10). A modern westerner might have started a new church with his awed followers as he cashed in on such great spiritual experiences! Some have done so. But Paul stayed Christ-centered, not experience-centered.

The troublemakers who manipulated the Christians in Corinth broke Paul's heart. If it was boasting they wanted, he could even boast about his sufferings for Christ's sake! (2 Cor. 11:24-29).

No matter what life brought, Paul had only one concern — that Jesus Christ be made known. "This priceless treasure we hold, so to speak, in a common earthenware jar — to show that the splendid power of it belongs to God and not to us. We are handicapped on all sides, but we are never frustrated; we are puzzled, but never in despair. We are persecuted but we never have to stand it alone: we may be knocked down but we are never knocked out! Every day we experience something of the death of Jesus, so that we may also know the power of the life of Jesus in these bodies of ours. . . . We are always facing death, but this means that you know more and more of life" (4:7-11 *Phillips*).

Because of his single-minded openness to God, Paul could truly say at the end of his life, "I have fought the good fight, I have finished the race, I have kept the faith" (2 Tim. 4:7).

He was, indeed, a "man in Christ," who calls us to the same life.

[1] Archibald Hunter, *The Gospel According to St. Paul* (Philadelphia: Westminster, 1967), p. 36.

[2] Gunther Bornkamm, *Paul* (New York: Harper & Row), p. 12; cf. Matthew 23:15.

[3] James Stewart, *A Man in Christ* (Grand Rapids: Baker, 1975), pp. 140, 141.

[4] Paul Tournier, *The Whole Person in a Broken World* (New York: Harper & Row, 1964), p. 156.

[5] Even though for years Paul's authorship of this letter was questioned, many respectable scholars do accept it. I like what Markus Barth said, that Paul did not need to be "Pauline," therefore the argument against his authorship is actually an argument for it.

[6] Karen Horney, *Neurosis and Human Growth* (New York: Norton, 1950), p. 155.

[7] Fritz Kunkel, *Creation Continues: A Study of the Gospel of Matthew* (Waco, TX: Word, 1973), pp. 122, 135.

14
PAUL, THE COUNSELOR

Even though Paul had times of ecstasy with the Lord, he was never intoxicated with these raptures. They never led to withdrawal, but always sent him forth to greater witnessing, not to his experiences but to the risen Lord. If he had not been pushed into a counseling situation, we would not even know about these experiences. His "visions and revelations of the Lord" (2 Cor. 12:1) and ecstasies induced by the Spirit (1 Cor. 14:8) he counted as private experiences (Rom. 8:26). His knowledge of Christ, from his conversion on through his life, he did not think of as unique and solitary, but from his own experience of the risen Lord he could witness to God's redemption through Christ.

Paul already knew that man in his own initiative and strength, no matter how religious he is, can only walk in self-centered circles. Paul did not just look back

171

to his encounter with the risen Lord; he walked with Him daily — by faith, as any Christian must. And the more the Lord meant to him, the more he was pressed to take the Good News to everyone else. "For necessity is laid upon me. Woe to me if I do not preach the gospel" (1 Cor. 9:16).

For Paul, "every one else" was not an impersonal mass of people. He understood and loved the people. When they were won to Christ, he carried concern for them on his heart as a parent carries concern for a loved child. His letters to these people were counseling letters, letters written to certain situations with the hope that these Christians would not lose Christ as the center of their lives and become enmeshed in peripheral things.

Perhaps no statement of Paul's is more misquoted than *"I have become all things to all men"* (1 Cor. 9:22). This is often quoted as an excuse for compromising, but this is a complete misreading of Paul's purpose and experience. He said,

> *For though I am free from all men, I have made myself a slave to all,* that I might win the more. *To the Jews I became as a Jew,* in order to win Jews; *to those under the law I became as one under the law — though not being myself under the law —* that I might win those under the law. *To those outside the law I became as one outside the law — not being without law toward God but* under the law of Christ — that I might win those outside the law. *To the weak I became weak,* that I might win the weak. *I have become all things to all men,* that I might by all means save some. I do it all for the

172

sake of the gospel, *that I may share its blessings (9:19-23).*

Paul was uncompromising when it came to anything about the supremacy of the Lord Jesus Christ; but in peripheral matters, even though important to him, he could make adjustments in order to win people to Christ.

This is the same kind of discernment I heard last summer about a Christian Catholic Church in Illinois. In this church the people are against eating pork. A member came one day to the second Overseer bishop in their history and said, "I like pork, I eat it. Will it keep me out of heaven?" The Overseer answered, "No, it won't keep you out of heaven; it will only get you there fifteen years sooner!"

As counselor Paul knew and understood his people, and he had mercy regarding their short-comings, even when he scolded them. He was heartbroken for the Galatians because they had been "bewitched" by legalists who told them they were second-rate Christians unless they followed the Jewish laws. He cried out to them, "Oh, my dear children, I feel the pangs of childbirth all over again till Christ be formed within you, and how I long to be with you now!" (Gal. 4:19,20 *Phillips).*

To the church at Philippi Paul wrote as friend to friend. His concern for them was that internal conflicts might arise to break the fellowship they had in Christ.

The church at Colossae was mixed up philosophically and theologically. They were displacing Christ as supreme and were mixed up on angelology. They also

173

had a tendency toward asceticism. Philemon was a rich member of this church, and he received a personal letter from Paul to accept his runaway slave as a brother in Christ.

The church at Thessalonica was so mixed up on the second coming of Christ that they wanted to quit all responsibility for livelihood. I guess we'd say they went on relief while they waited. They had been severely persecuted and needed encouragement to steadfastness. They also needed renewed teaching on purity in life; the body is not for self-gratification. "You cannot break this rule without in some way cheating your fellow-men" (1 Thess. 4:6).

To the Ephesians Paul wrote an ecumenical letter about the ultimate and most dependable things in life and about the most hidden things in God's universe. Dr. John A. Mackay calls this letter the "music of faith" and the distilled essence of the Christian religion.[1]

Paul also wrote a letter to a church he did not yet know — the one at Rome. Phoebe, a deaconess in the church at Cenchraeae, was about to sail for Rome, so he wrote this treatise on salvation through Jesus Christ and sent it with her.

All these letters have discernments on what is *authentic experience of God*, but the correspondence with the Corinthian church really probes into this subtle problem of "religious experience." The Gentiles in this city were very religious before they became Christians, and they were prone to fall back into old culture patterns because their consciences had not yet been

174

fully retrained. We cannot understand Paul's letters to them unless we know something about these people to whom he wrote. Paul was thinking of *them;* he was *not* thinking of us centuries later. But people are the same the ages through and the world around, and much of the letter sounds as though he is writing to us in our day.

It has been said that Corinth was made for greatness. The city was on an isthmus between two good seaports. The Greek city was destroyed in 146 B.C. by the Romans and rebuilt by Julius Caesar in 46 B.C. as a Roman colony, which became the capital of Achaia. In Paul's day it was a new city with few traditions; it was a commercial city engrossed in making money. Its population was made up of Roman veterans, merchants, hucksters, Jews and Gentiles of all kinds, and thousands of slaves, not even counted in the census. It was famous for its bronze which was unrivaled in its beauty, made so by female slaves who were forced to polish it with their bare arms until their skin was gone. Corinth was also famous for its pottery. But Corinth's greatest notoriety was from its immorality sanctioned by its religion. Visiting sailors and merchants did not expect to get out of the city with much money left. To call a person a Corinthian anywhere in Greece or Italy was to say he was immoral or a drunkard.

There were temples in this city to Heracles, Poseidon, Apollo, Hermes, Jupiter, Octavia, Asclepius, and Aphrodite. Of most interest to us as background for Corinthian church problems are the temples of Asclepius and Aphrodite. Asclepius was the god of healing and health (father of Hygeia). As this temple was excavated, all kinds of terra-cotta organs and parts of the body were found. Whenever anyone was healed, he had an image of the healed part made and offered it at the temple.

The most famous temple in Corinth was the temple of Aphrodite on the top of the mountain called Acrocorinth, which rose 1,750 feet above the city. Aphrodite was the goddess of love, the mother of Cupid, and she had a thousand priestesses in her temple for the benefit of all male worshipers. These were all beautiful girls, religious prostitutes, and men came from everywhere to ''worship''! At evening time these priestesses came down into the city and accosted the men on the street. It became a Greek proverb: ''It is not every man who can afford a journey to Corinth.'' In writing to the church there, as Paul lists all the evil kinds of people who cannot enter the kingdom of God, he adds, ''and such were some of you'' (1 Cor. 6:11).

One wonders how Paul could have had the courage to preach the gospel in such a wicked city. But he started in the Jewish synagogue where he felt at home — for a while — until they put him out; then he went next door to the home of Titius Justus who worshiped God. Many people became believers and were baptized. As opposition grew, the Lord came to Paul one night in a vision and said to him, ''Do not be afraid, but speak and do not be silent; for I am with you, and no man shall attack you to harm you; for I have many people in this city'' (Acts 18:9,10). Paul stayed there a year and six months, and a church was established in this evil ''inner city.''

The membership list is interesting — Titius Justus; Crispus, the former synagogue ruler (Acts 18:8; 1 Cor. 1:14); Erastus, the city treasurer (Romans 16:23; Acts 19:22); Aquila and Priscilla with whom Paul lived; Stephanus, the first convert (1 Cor. 1:16; 16:15); Gaius (1 Cor. 1:14; Romans 16:23); Chloe (1 Cor. 1:11); Phoebe (Rom. 16:1); the poor (1 Cor. 1:26-28); slaves (1 Cor. 7:22); dockyard workers; small tradesmen; free men; Jews; and Gentiles. Every social class was there together in one church!

No wonder there were problems in that social mixture. The first problem concerned cliques and factions (1 Cor. 1:10-17; 3:3-15). But it is interesting to note that these cliques were not arranged according to cultural conditions but according to which preacher they idolized. Some said, "I belong to Paul," or "I belong to Apollos," or "I belong to Cephas." And others came along and claimed to be the spiritual ones. They said, "We belong to Christ." Paul wanted them to know that such quarreling did not belong to Christ's people. Christ was not divided.

The next big problem in the church at Corinth was immorality (1 Cor. 5). This is not surprising considering the background of most of the members. What Paul taught these new Christians was the "new morality" of that day. (The so-called "new morality" of today is older than that sex temple on the Acrocorinth! Paul's teaching is still the new morality.) Because of the new freedom experienced in the Christian fellowship, these babes in Christ were not yet responsible in their freedom, and so they even did what was considered immoral in immoral Corinth. The church was responsible in this situation because they were indifferent to this evil in their midst. They should have used discipline so the sinning one could be redeemed.

These babes in Christ were also displaying their grievances with one another in pagan courts. This was no Christian witness. They should have been concerned for one another and sacrificed even their rights for Christ's sake (6:1-8).

The discipline of the love of God was new, so they fell back into their old culture and religious patterns. They were still in the midst of religious prostitution. Perhaps many of the Christians were approached by those beautiful girls as they came down into the town in the evening. "If they were really spiritual, what did it matter what the body did?" Paul said it did matter. "Do you not know that your body is a temple of the Holy Spirit within you, which you have from God? You are not your own; you were bought with a price. So glorify God in your body" (6:19,20). This temptation is so subtle that Christians still get caught.

The problems so far had been reported to Paul, but he also had a letter from the church asking about other matters. They wanted to know how a real experience of Christ would relate to these matters. The first one of these was in relation to marriage. They had many detailed questions ranging from such ascetic attitudes that even husband and wife should avoid sex relations in order to be "spiritual" to the other extreme of unfaithfulness. The new thing for Corinth (and perhaps for us, too) was that Paul in Christ gave man and

178

woman the same status: "For the wife does not rule over her own body, but the husband does; *likewise* the husband does not rule over his own body, but the wife does" (7:4). The first half of this statement followed the accepted pattern, but the second half meant a revolution! This was according to Paul's main thesis that in Christ there is neither male nor female (Gal. 3:28). Without question, some of the other things Paul said were because he expected the second coming of Christ to be imminent. In fact, he gave that as his reason for possible avoidance of marriage.

Another big question for the Christians in Corinth was concerning the matter of meat which had been sacrificed to idols (1 Cor. 8). Almost any meat bought in the market might have been that kind. For new Christians who had bought such meat as part of idol worship, it might have been a pull back into old ways of worship. For Paul it meant nothing at all. He could eat it or not eat it. But Paul said the real issue was personal freedom in relation to others and to Christ.

Christian freedom is paradoxical. Paul said, "For though I am free from all men, I have made myself a slave to all, that I might win the more" (9:19). J. Stanley Glen says, "The special significance of the paradoxical derives entirely from Christ as the definitive norm. Freedom *from* men means freedom *for* Christ — in the peculiar manner in which Paul is bound to him as his slave. But just because he is the slave of Christ he is thereby enabled to become a slave to men without becoming enslaved to them. In this respect he is free *for* them. Thus, the one freedom which is indica-

179

tive of separation *from,* and therefore ultimately of holiness, is cognate to the other freedom, which is indicative of separation unto (identification), and therefore is indicative ultimately of love."[2] We will soon see how relative this kind of freedom is to the tests for true experience of God.

Self-centeredness, which is a biblical definition of sin, even spoiled the fellowship at the Lord's Supper (10:14-22; 11:17-34). Paul had to tell them they were worse off for having met in this church meeting! (11:17). "When you meet together, it is not the Lord's supper that you eat. For in eating, *each one goes ahead with his own meal"* (11:20). One can be religious enough to go through the forms of his worship and still miss in his relationship to Christ. "So that, whoever eats the bread or drinks the cup of the Lord without proper reverence" is like one of those who allowed the Lord to be put to death without discerning who He was. "No, a man should thoroughly examine himself, and only then should he eat the bread or drink the cup. He that eats and drinks carelessly is eating and drinking a judgment on himself, for he is blind to the presence of the Lord's body" (11:27-29 *Phillips).* It is important to test one's self for authenticity in one's relationship to God and to others.

With all their religiosity, the strangest conflict in the Corinthian church was their competitiveness in relation to their spiritual gifts. They forgot the difference between the *gift* of the Holy Spirit and the *gifts* of the Spirit. The same immature self-centeredness was revealed as they argued about which gift was preeminent. Paul didn't want them to be uninformed about these spiritual gifts (1 Cor. 12–14). F. B. Meyer said, "When we discuss what we believe we are divided, but when we discuss whom we believe we come together." This the Corinthian church had not learned yet; they were still divided.

The first test for an authentic experience of the Holy Spirit is when one can truly say, "Jesus is Lord." For Paul it meant the indwelling Christ (12:3). This is what Jesus meant when He told about the coming of the Spirit: "He will glorify me, for he will take what is mine and declare it to you" (John 16:14). Any witness that glorifies one's self is arrogant witness, and therefore it becomes divisive. In Christ we can never say, "Unless your experience is like mine, you do not have the real thing."

So Paul says there are *varieties of gifts,* but the same Lord (1 Cor. 12:8-11).

This is true individuation. Only in Christ can the creative powers of any individual be truly fulfilled. The more of Christ through the Holy Spirit, the greater the difference between individuals. No one is ever a copy of another. Each is free to be his best and highest self. It is just like the body which is made up of different parts; every part is important for its own function.

Not only do individual experiences differ, but *each manifestation of the Spirit is given for the common good* (12:7). This is the story from Abraham to Paul. God calls to make the one responsive to Him a *blessing* to others. Religious self-centeredness is worse than the selfishness of the person who makes no religious pro-

181

fession. Religious self-centeredness, or pride, keeps other people from the Lord. A true manifestation in one's life sets one free to minister to others, to understand them and to love them.

This leads to the second test Paul gave for an authentic experience of Christ in the fullness of the Spirit. Rather than being argumentative about rating different experiences, Paul showed a more excellent way, the way of love. This word was formerly translated "charity," but the word *charity* has lost its real meaning. And love is too often thought of today as Aphrodite would have used it, therefore many Christians use the Greek word *agape*. Of the four Greek words for love, this one was seldom used. It was left clean for Christian usage. Agape demands the exercise of the whole man. Such a love is bound to be a product of the Spirit. Christian *agape* is impossible for anyone except a Christian.

If we keep this Greek meaning in mind, we can better understand what the Corinthian church heard when Paul's letter was read to them.

Without this love, an experience of tongues or prophecy was worth nothing. Without it, knowledge and even faith were of no significance. Without this love, giving away everything for others or giving one's body to be burned would bring no gain whatever. *Agape* love is the identifying mark of the true believer.

With this understanding of love, we can take our own examination by substituting *I* for *love* in the thirteenth chapter of 1 Corinthians:

I am patient and kind;
I am not jealous or boastful;
I am not arrogant or rude.
I do not insist on my own way;
I am not irritable or resentful;
I do not rejoice at wrong;
I rejoice in the right.
I bear all things;
I believe all things;
I hope all things;
I endure all things.

Indeed, this is possible only in Christ through the Holy Spirit. Love is the *movement* of the Holy Spirit and the test of an authentic experience of God. Jesus said, "By this all men will know that you are my disciples, if you have love for one another" (John 13:35).

Then Paul went back to his discussion on the gifts of the Spirit, especially the speaking in tongues with the admonition to "Make love your aim" (1 Cor. 14:1). He made no case *for* or *against* speaking in tongues. His only concern was for the people to put Christ and love first.

My husband and I have a dear friend, a missionary. I have heard him say more than once, "If you seek tongues, you will never find the Lord. Seek the Lord and take whatever He gives you." This is what Paul meant in "Make love your aim" and "Since you are eager for manifestations of the Spirit, strive to excel in building up the church" (14:12). Paul himself rejoiced in this experience — privately. Some have suggested that this is what he meant in Romans 8:26: "Likewise the Spirit helps us in our weakness; for we do not know how to pray as we ought, but the Spirit himself intercedes for us with sighs too deep for words."

To the Corinthians Paul said, "I thank God that I speak in tongues more than you all; nevertheless, in church I would rather speak five words with my mind, in order to instruct others, than ten thousand words in a tongue" (1 Cor. 14:18,19). The reason for this was: "He who speaks in a tongue edifies himself, but he who prophesies edifies the church" (14:4). Actually, the issue in Corinth was not for or against speaking in tongues, but whether their religious experiences were in the *Lord* and whether they were loving.

To Paul the question was: Did the Corinthians want religious experience as an end in itself, or did they want an experience of Christ through the Holy Spirit? This problem is as modern as today. Recently I was handed a written question in a meeting: "Do you go along with coaching people into voicing syllables to help them to receive the gift of tongues?" This is the very issue Paul was speaking to — the difference between a real gift from God when seeking Christ only or a human striving to get a religious experience.

This was the real issue in Corinth. The Corinthians knew about healings in the temple to Asclepius. (Faith itself has healing power up to a certain point.) They knew about prophecy. The muses who were guardians at Delphi had the gift of prophecy: "They said that which is, what will be, and what has been."[3] They also knew about tongues at Delphi.

There was a place where certain gases came out from the ground. Women were forcibly held over these places, sitting on a tripod, and there "received the prophetic exhalations. Their faces paled, their limbs shook with convulsive movements. At first they uttered only whimpering complaints and groans; soon, with gleaming eyes and foaming mouth, their hair on end with fright, they were heard to speak, amidst cries of pain, broken incoherent words, recorded with care and painstakingly put into verse by a priest, himself taken in by his faith in the oracle who had to discover the revelation of the future as hidden in these words by the god."[4] This manipulated experience is the kind of religious experience Paul was warning against.

Paul touched the key to the difference between a Christ experience in religious ecstasy and the pagan way when he said, "Brethren, do not be children in your thinking; be babes in evil, but in thinking be mature" (1 Cor. 14:20). Then he discussed the orderliness which should prevail in a Christian service which may include "a hymn, a lesson, a revelation, a tongue, or an interpretation. Let all things be done for edification. . . . For God is not a God of confusion but of peace" (14:26,33). By emphasizing the use of one's mind and maintaining the freedom of human choice, Paul was really saying that the closer to God one is, even in an ecstatic experience, the freer the human will is. This was never true in pagan religious ecstasy. It is not true in any humanly contrived experience.

In this connection I must add that I believe that the times when we do not consciously know we are guided

185

are even greater evidence of the Spirit's presence in our unconscious, if you please, than the times we have direction *ahead* of time — so near is the Lord to us when He dwells in our hearts and minds.

The women were a definite part of the confusion in the Corinthian church. The women who became Christian had never had such freedom before (Neither male nor female in Christ!), and they did not yet know how to use their freedom. Paul had to chide them: ''What! Did the word of God originate with you, or are you the only ones it has reached?'' (14:36).

The church also had questions about the Resurrection. Paul had to go back to his basic teaching when he first came to them: ''Now I would remind you, brethren, in what terms I preached to you the gospel, which you received, in which you stand, by which you are saved, *if you hold it fast* — unless you believed in vain. For I delivered to you as of *first importance* what I also received, that Christ died for our sins in accordance with the scriptures, that he was buried, that he was raised on the third day in accordance with the scriptures'' (5:1-4), and then Paul gives a list of the appearances. All the appearances listed were to the disciples before the Ascension, except the appearance to Paul which came after the Ascension. To Paul this meant that Christ was indeed a living Lord, a contemporary Presence, seen or unseen, the indwelling Christ, the fullness of the Holy Spirit.

Even though Paul counted himself unworthy, he could with a whole heart say, ''It is through the love of God that I am what I am, and the love which he showed me has not been wasted" (1 Cor. 15:10 *Twentieth Century*). Paul is one person who did not waste the love of God; he let it flow through him to all the people whom he loved for Christ's sake.

Paul longed to visit Rome. When he finally went there, he went as a prisoner. He didn't even have to pay his own way! (Acts 27; 28). Paul was permitted to live in a rented house at his own expense for two years — but as a prisoner. Christians and many others came to see him and found the Lord through him. It is to our advantage that he was imprisoned, because he had time to write letters to those he loved, and we share in those letters. He wrote to Timothy, "For I am already on the point of being sacrificed; the time of my departure has come. I have fought the good fight, I have finished the race, I have kept the faith" (2 Tim. 4:6,7).

Legend tells us that Paul was beheaded outside the city of Rome, where many other Christians were persecuted and killed.

Paul's monument is in his faith, preserved in the letters he wrote.

[1]John A. Mackay, *God's Order,* p. 17.

[2]J. Stanley Glen, *Pastoral Problems in First Corinthians,* p. 121.

[3]*New Larouse Encyclopedia of Mythology* (Buffalo, NY: Prometheus Books), p. 119.

[4]Victory Durur, *The World of the Greeks,* p. 69.

15
THE GOD OF THE NOW

We complete our journey through the Bible with a book called Revelation. And it is revelation if we look for its real meaning. Most books end with a final statement *The End*, but the Bible closes with a message of a new *beginning*. From Genesis to Revelation there is always *expectation* for the *something more* the heavenly Father is ready to do for us. No matter what happens there is always *hope*.

God created man in His own image, which means man was created with the capacity to have fellowship with an unseen God. But since God did not want mere puppets, He created man with the responsibility of choice. And man chose disobedience. So sin entered the world. The Creator, who *is love*, promised man that choice was still available for redemption.

Man remained religious because he was created to

have communion with God, but in his self-centeredness he thought he could manage his worship himself and make his own gods. But God got through to Abraham and chose a people to represent Him and to tell His plan of redemption from sin. Through the centuries people were so slow to learn that a real God loved them and could give them new life.

Most of the people did not hear, even the people whom God had specially chosen to represent Him. So He came among us Himself in the person of His Son, Jesus of Nazareth, a real human being and also the Son of God. He was the first human to have perfect communion with God, the Creator of all the earth. Jesus lived among us so we could know what the God of love and forgiveness is really like. Of course, men killed Him, as they had killed the prophets before Him. But they could not get rid of Jesus. (Remember, it was the orthodoxy of that day that wanted Him out of the way. We must be careful to find the true orthodoxy.) Glorious, triumphant news! He arose from the tomb, and He is present with us even to this day through His Holy Spirit.

That is the message of the last book of the Bible: *He is alive!* Most people think that the Book of Revelation is inscrutable. Others spend all their energies using it as a kind of celestial timetable of the future. But it was written especially for seven churches in Asia (Rev. 1:11). Those churches were much like our churches today, and they serve as a mirror for us. (Which church is yours like?) They had problems and trouble, but they were told that the living Lord was with them. From

Creation to the end of the age, the greatest truth of life is that we need not despair; we can have *hope*. When Jesus, the risen Lord, ascended from earth, the message that followed was that He would return (Acts 1:11).

Recently a young man said to me, "My problem is that I have no goal in life." He already knew he was successful as the world counts success, but he had finally run into something he could not manage because it involved others and their choices. This is the same reason many people do not understand the Bible. They do not see the goal for man and nations as revealed in God's Word.

Our history is still God's history. God will bring to a conclusion His goal in human history, and He needs our obedience and cooperation.

There was no committee with a secretary sitting to observe the creation of the world. It was ages later when God's people were inspired to write the story. You have heard it said, "These things are true because they are in the Bible." I think it is more accurate to say they are in the Bible because they are true. That would help us avoid the points on which people quibble, and it would leave us free to find the central message of God's Word. The writers of the Bible were telling us that God did create the world, but not how He did it. We will not stumble then because Old Testament people did not know all of God's will. That is why Jesus had to come. Remember always that God is the hero of the Bible, not imperfect man.

Faith? It is first of all to be placed in God, a personal God who created us, who loves us enough to forgive us no matter what condition we find ourselves in, who takes the initiative toward us, who sent His Son to save us and give us abundant life. We read the Bible to meet God. If we do not meet Him, we have not heard the message of the Bible. Life is available because the same God still lives. Through Jesus Christ we know Him; through the Holy Spirit He is present with us and in us when we give ourselves completely to Him. No other faith has such *amazing grace* available.

We need never fear to trust God and what He wants for us. Many people are deterred from turning to God because they have the foolish notion, gained from the attitude of some church members, that all God says is "No, no." But in Christianity, prohibitions are only against those things which lead to grief and death. Jesus came to bring abundant life. This is the wonder of the Bible message.

In this generation we have watched men walk on the moon; we have heard an astronaut's heartbeat through all-intervening space. All this was possible because laws of the universe were obeyed. No one called those laws prohibitions. And God created that universe. God's laws in any sphere set people free for unbelievable accomplishments. The spiritual laws of personality make even greater liberation possible.

The Bible is our textbook for life. Our part is to read and obey.

POSTSCRIPT

Bibliography and *Bible* come from the same root word. There are plenty of books to help you understand the Bible, but the Bible itself is the best help. Of course, you must learn how to read it. Just taking individual texts is not enough, no matter how wonderful they are. Read whole books at one sitting. This is the opposite of "proof-texting" — using certain texts to prove one's own ideas. By beginning with the belief that *God is,* then reading His Word with a listening ear, God will be able to speak to you as He did to His people so long ago.

Someone said the Bible is the best selling but least read of all books. Perhaps that is changing now that we have so many versions in our everyday language.

Read and read. You will be thrilled, convicted, and comforted. Obey what God the heavenly Father shows you, and you will have the greatest adventure of your life.

because he was the only father Mya would ever know. I signed my name on the consent form and handed the clipboard back to Clint.

"She's been my life from the moment I knew I was pregnant." For whatever reason, I needed Clint to know I was a good mother. I hadn't used the baby's Enfamil to mix a White Russian before noon or added a couple of Benadryl drops to Mya's bottle to get her to fall asleep. I'd avoided many of the offenses I'd heard about from the other mommies in the playgroup, though I admit to giving their suggestions a bit of thought.

"The accident was awful. The guy came out of nowhere," I said, trying to keep my focus on his eyes instead of on the perfect form of his lips.

"She's going to be fine." Clint broke the awkward silence. "So what about you? How're you holding up?"

"My face hurts. My ribs hurt," I said, wiping the stupid tear, then the second one steaming off my cheek. "I can't feel anything in my leg except itchy-scratchy. This robe makes me feel overexposed, and my nurses were trained at the Sumo Wrestler Nursing Academy. Other than that, I'm fine."

"Good, what I like to hear."

I spat bubbles from laughter. The morphine left me a bit loose. I hoped I hadn't given too much information, like *Damn, he looked good*. But hadn't he always? Hadn't he been the one that got away, at least in my mind?

"I'm the head of Pediatrics here. I'm on the advisory board, too," he said, waiting for me to clap like a seal for his accomplishments.

"I guess Kaiser knows a good thing when they see it."

"No, Jackson Memorial," he corrected.

I sucked in all the available air in the room. "I'm at Jackson Memorial?"

Clint nodded his head up and down. "Jack the Ripper" was a well-known epithet in Los Angeles County. The hospital in the hood was known for doing more harm than good. Emergency victims left dying in the aisles. Doctors with good intentions but overworked with only half the pay. I swallowed hard.

He frowned, knowing what I was thinking. "Jackson was the only trauma center open. Trust me, you're in good hands."

"Ah-huh," I said, looking for the nearest exit.

"I know what people say, but it's not true. This hospital is special."

Understatement.

"All it took was one look at the babies in Neonatal, and I couldn't walk away. Kandi was especially concerned. She thought my career was doomed once I signed on to a place like Jackson Memorial."

The mere mention of Kandi's name made my stomach boil. Kandi married Clint on the rebound after I'd kicked him to the curb. The curb was supposed to be temporary, teach him a lesson not to take advantage of the hand that fed him. A hard lesson that turned out to be mine. She wasted no time seducing Clint and carrying him off by his britches. She took him home, fed him a bunch of bullshit until he was stuffed, wiped his mouth, belched him, and said, there, there, you'll not have to be bothered by that nasty Venus again.

I beat myself up about the fact that I let a good man go—a doctor, no less. But once I saw clearly, I knew Clint and I were never meant to be together. Didn't mean I agreed with his choice. Kandi was a gold digger with long legs and big breasts and the determination of a long-distance track runner. She wanted Clint and she got him.